The New

P O C K E T

Factfile

of the

WORLD

Vineyard Books

Cartographic Manager: Richard Watts
Cartographic Editors: Polly Senior,
    Tim Williams
Project Editor: Fiona Gold
Designer: Frankie Wood
Proof reader: Lin Thomas
Production: Clive Sparling

Vineyard Books is an imprint of
Andromeda Oxford Ltd.

 Planned and produced by
Andromeda Oxford Ltd
11–15 The Vineyard
Abingdon
Oxfordshire OX14 3PX

© copyright Andromeda Oxford Ltd 1996

All rights reserved. No part of this
publication may be reproduced, stored
in a retrieval system, or transmitted, in
any form or by any means, electronic,
mechanical, photocopying, recording or
otherwise, without the permission of
the publisher.

ISBN 1-871869-70-6

Origination by Pixel Tech Ltd., Singapore

Flags produced by Lovell Johns, Oxford,
UK, and authenticated by The Flag
Research Center, Winchester, Mass.
01890, USA, and by The Flag Institute,
10 Vicarage Road, Chester CH2 3HZ,
England.

Printed by Tien Wah Press, Singapore

CONTENTS

CONTENTS (continued)

FACTFILE OF THE WORLD

GLOBAL INFORMATION

	Area	
	sq km	sq mi
The World	509,450,000	196,672,000
Water	360,000,000	138,984,000
Land	149,450,000	57,688,000
Asia	44,500,000	17,177,000
Africa	30,302,000	11,697,000
North America	24,241,000	9,357,000
South America	17,793,000	6,868,000
Antarctica	14,100,000	5,443,000
Europe	9,957,000	3,843,000
Australasia & Oceania	8,557,000	3,303,000

OCEANS

	Area	
	sq km	sq mi
Pacific Ocean	179,679,000	69,356,000
Atlantic Ocean	92,373,000	35,657,000
Indian Ocean	73,917,000	28,532,000
Arctic Ocean	14,090,000	5,439,000

LARGEST SEAS

	Area	
	sq km	sq mi
Caribbean	2,766,000	1,068,000
Mediterranean	2,516,000	971,000
South China Sea	2,318,000	895,000
Bering Sea	2,268,000	875,000
Gulf of Mexico	1,543,000	596,000
Sea of Okhotsk	1,528,000	590,000
East China and Yellow Sea	1,249,000	482,000
Hudson Bay	1,232,000	476,000
Sea of Japan	1,008,000	389,000
North Sea	575,000	223,000
Black Sea	452,000	174,000
Red Sea	438,000	169,000
Baltic Sea	397,000	153,000
Persian Gulf	239,000	92,000
Gulf of St. Lawrence	238,000	92,500
Gulf of California	162,000	62,500
Bass Strait	75,000	29,000

HIGHEST MOUNTAINS

	Location	Height	
		m	ft
Everest	Nepal	8,848	29,028
K2	Pakistan	8,611	28,250
Kanchenjunga	India	8,598	28,208
Lhotse 1	China	8,516	27,939
Makalu	China	8,481	27,824
Cho Oyu	China	8,201	26,906
Dhaulgiri	Nepal	8,172	26,811
Manaslu	Nepal	8,156	26,758
Nanga Parbat	Pakistan	8,126	26,660
Annapurna	Nepal	8,078	26,502
Gasherbrum	China	8,068	26,469
Mount Broad	India	8,051	26,414
Gosainthan	China	8,012	26,286

LOWEST POINTS

	Location	Depth below sea level	
		m	ft
Dead Sea	Asia	-400	-1,312
Turfan Depression	China	-154	-505
Lake Assal	Djibouti	-150	-492
Mangyshlak Depression	Kazakhstan	-132	-433
Death Valley	N. America	-86	-282

LONGEST RIVERS

	Length	
	km	mi
Nile	6,690	4,160
Amazon	6,570	4,080
Mississippi-Missouri	6,020	3,740
Yangtze	5,900	3,722
Yenisey	5,870	3,650
Ob-Irtysh	5,410	3,360
Huang	4,840	3,005
Zaire	4,630	2,880
Amur	4,510	2,800
Paraná	4,500	2,800
Lena	4,400	2,730

LARGEST LAKES

	Location	Area sq km	sq mi
Caspian Sea	Asia	371,000	143,000
Lake Superior	Canada/USA	83,270	32,150
Aral Sea	Kazakhstan	66,500	25,700
Lake Victoria	East Africa	62,940	24,300
Lake Huron	Canada/USA	59,600	23,000
Lake Michigan	USA	58,000	22,400
Lake Tanganyika	Central Africa	32,900	12,700
Great Bear Lake	Canada	31,500	12,200
Lake Baikal	Russia	31,500	12,200
Lake Malawi	East Africa	29,600	11,400
Great Slave Lake	Canada	28,700	11,100
Lake Erie	Canada/USA	25,700	9,900
Lake Chad	Central Africa	25,000	9,700
Lake Winnipeg	Canada	24,400	9,400
Lake Ontario	Canada/USA	19,500	7,500
Lake Balkhash	Kazakhstan	18,500	7,100
Lake Ladoga	Russia	18,400	7,100
Tonle Sap	Cambodia	10,000	3,860
Lake Eyre	Australia	9,000	3,500

LARGEST ISLANDS

	Area sq km	sq mi
Australia	7,682,300	2,966,200
Greenland	2,175,600	839,800
New Guinea	780,000	301,080
Borneo	737,000	284,000
Madagascar	587,041	226,658
Baffin Island	508,000	196,100
Sumatra	425,000	164,000
Honshu	230,000	88,800
Great Britain	229,880	88,700
Victoria I.	212,200	81,900
Ellesmere I.	212,000	81,800
Sulawesi	189,000	73,000
New Zealand (S)	150,500	58,100
Java	126,700	48,900
Cuba	110,861	42,804
New Zealand (N)	114,400	44,200
Luzon	104,700	40,400

MOST POPULOUS COUNTRIES

	Population for 1994
China	1,190,431,106
India	919,903,056
United States	260,713,000
Indonesia	200,409,745
Brazil	158,739,257
Russia	149,609,000
Pakistan	128,856,000
Bangladesh	125,149,469
Japan	125,106,937
Nigeria	92,800,000
Mexico	92,202,199

LARGEST CITIES

	Population for 1994
Mexico City, Mexico	13,636,000
Bombay, India	12,572,000
Shanghai, China	12,320,000
Tokyo, Japan	11,936,000
Buenos Aires, Argentina	11,256,000
Calcutta, India	10,916,000
Seoul, South Korea	10,628,000
Beijing, China	9,750,000
Sao Paulo, Brazil	9,627,000
Paris, France	9,319,000

PRINCIPAL LANGUAGES

	Number of speakers (1991)
Chinese	845,000,000
English	485,000,000
Hindustani	338,000,000
Spanish	331,000,000
Russian	291,000,000
Arabic	192,000,000
Bengali	181,000,000
Portuguese	171,000,000
Malay Indonesian	138,000,000
Japanese	124,000,000
German	118,000,000
French	117,000,000
Urdu	90,000,000

THE POLITICAL WORLD

Greenland (Denmark)

Svalbard (Norway)

ICELAND

SWEDEN
FINLAND
NORWAY
ESTONIA
LATVIA
UNITED
KINGDOM DEN
IRELAND N
POL
BEL
CZ
LUX
FRANCE SW
AN
PORTUGAL SPAIN
ITALY
GREECE
MALTA
TUNISIA
MOROCCO
ALGERIA
LIBYA
Western Sahara (Morocco)
MAURITANIA
MALI
NIGER
CHAD
CAPE VERDE
SENEGAL
GA
G.B. GUINEA
B.F.
BE
IVORY
COAST G
NIGERIA
SIERRA LEONE
LIBERIA
CAMEROON
C.A.R.
SÃO TOMÉ & PRÍNCIPE
EQ
GABON
CONGO
Cabinda (Angola)
ZAIRE
ANGOLA
ZAMBIA
NAMIBIA
BOTSWANA
SOUTH AFRICA

CANADA

UNITED STATES
OF AMERICA

BAHAMAS
CUBA
MEXICO
DOM.
GUATEMALA BELIZE J. HA.
A.B.
HONDURAS
S.K. D.
EL SALVADOR NICARAGUA
S.L.
S.V. BAR.
COSTA RICA
GR. T.T.
PANAMA VENEZUELA
COLOMBIA GUYANA
SURINAME
French Guiana (France)
ECUADOR

PERU
BRAZIL

BOLIVIA
PARAGUAY
CHILE

URUGUAY
ARGENTINA

A.	AUSTRIA
A.B.	ANTIGUA AND BARBUDA
AL.	ALBANIA
AN.	ANDORRA
AR.	ARMENIA
AZ.	AZERBAIJAN
B.	BOSNIA HERZEGOVINA
BA.	BAHRAIN
BANG.	BANGLADESH
BAR.	BARBADOS
BEL.	BELGIUM
BE.	BENIN
B.F.	BURKINA FASO
BU.	BURUNDI
C.	CROATIA
C.A.R.	CENTRAL AFRICAN REPUBLIC
CYP.	CYPRUS
CZ.	CZECH REPUBLIC
D.	DOMINICA

DEN.	DENMARK
DJ.	DJIBOUTI
DOM.	DOMINICAN REPUBLIC
E.	ERITREA
EQ.	EQUATORIAL GUINEA
G.	GHANA
GA.	GAMBIA
G.B.	GUINEA-BISSAU
GE.	GEORGIA
GER.	GERMANY
GR.	GRENADA
H.	HUNGARY
HA.	HAITI
J.	JAMAICA
K.	KUWAIT
L.	LEBANON
LITH.	LITHUANIA
LUX.	LUXEMBOURG
M.	FORMER YUGOSLAV REPUBLIC OF MACEDONIA

N.	NETHERLANDS
POL.	POLAND
Q.	QATAR
R.	RUSSIA
RW.	RWANDA
S.	SLOVENIA
SIN.	SINGAPORE
S.K.	ST. KITTS-NEVIS
SL.	SLOVAKIA
S.L.	ST. LUCIA
S.V.	ST. VINCENT AND THE GRENADINES
SW.	SWITZERLAND
T.	TOGO
TA.	TAJIKISTAN
T.T.	TRINIDAD AND TOBAGO
TURK.	TURKMENISTAN
U.A.E.	UNITED ARAB EMIRATES
YU.	YUGOSLAVIA
ZIM.	ZIMBABWE

THE PHYSICAL WORLD

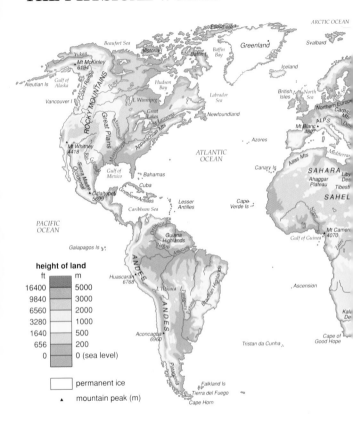

Land covers over 149,000,000 sq km (over 57,000,000 sq mi) of the Earth's surface, and can be divided broadly into physical regions, whose features are shaped by mountains, valleys and rivers. These features are changing constantly in response to dramatic forces such as earthquakes or volcanic eruptions; or slow forces such as erosion caused by running water, ocean waves, wind, or ice. The dramatic forces work inside the Earth, as movements in the

partly molten mantle that lies under the Earth's lithosphere, the outer shell made up of huge blocks called tectonic plates. As the plates move they cause earthquakes or volcanic eruptions, creating new valleys and mountains. By contrast, much of the rock worn away by the slower forces of erosion is dumped on the sea bed, or along the beds of rivers and lakes, where it piles up and, after years under pressure, forms new rock layers.

THE WORLD'S VEGETATION

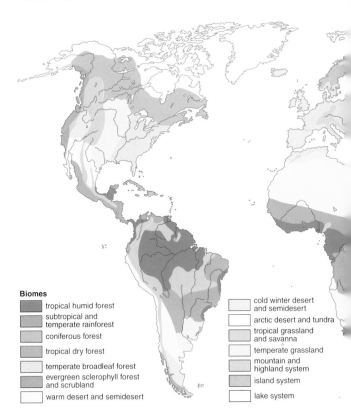

Biomes

- tropical humid forest
- subtropical and temperate rainforest
- coniferous forest
- tropical dry forest
- temperate broadleaf forest
- evergreen sclerophyll forest and scrubland
- warm desert and semidesert
- cold winter desert and semidesert
- arctic desert and tundra
- tropical grassland and savanna
- temperate grassland
- mountain and highland system
- island system
- lake system

Scientists have divided the world's vegetation into 14 categories called biomes. A biome describes the type of plant and animal communities (grassland, rainforest, desert etc) that would flourish in a given area if it was left undisturbed. Special biomes are associated with mountains, lakes and islands. Biomes change constantly, through natural forces or human interference, and some are very short lived. For example, lakes silt up and turn into

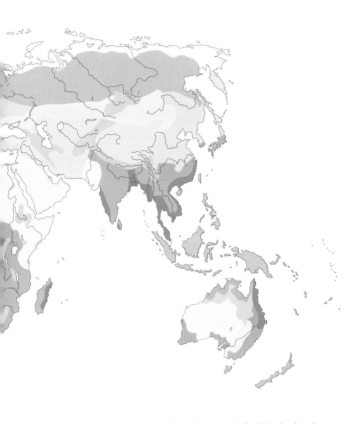

marshes; the existing plants and animals adapt, and new species florish in the altered environment. Over a longer timescale the marsh may become dry land. Many of the flat expanses of the western United States, for example, were once lakes. Human influence is felt mostly in the destruction of tropical forest. Over the next 25–50 years experts predict that one quarter of the world's species face extinction through destruction of biomes.

THE WORLD'S AGRICULTURE

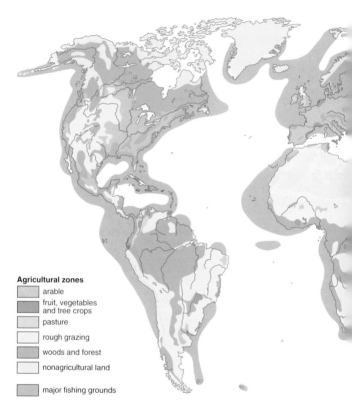

Agricultural zones

- arable
- fruit, vegetables and tree crops
- pasture
- rough grazing
- woods and forest
- nonagricultural land

- major fishing grounds

Agriculture produces a large percentage of the world's food, and provides raw materials for a variety of other industries including textiles, paper making and cosmetics. Climate and soil type tend to control the type of agriculture practiced in any region, though irrigation has made some dry areas highly productive. Areas that receive high rainfall and have good drainage are reserved for arable farming or pasture for cattle, with dryer areas being used to rear goats and sheep, which can survive on rough grazing. In most prosperous societies

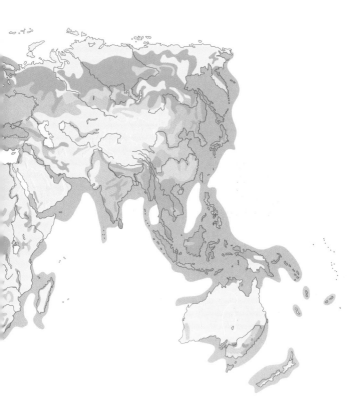

agriculture employs a tiny percentage of the work force. The United States is the world's largest food producer, but agriculture employs only 3 percent of the work force. Much of US produce is sold abroad, with modern transportation, and refrigeration methods making most crops viable for export. In developing countries, however, the majority of the population works on the land. Most agriculture is at subsistence level, with each smallholding producing just enough for the family or local community with little left over for sale.

THE WORLD'S POPULATION

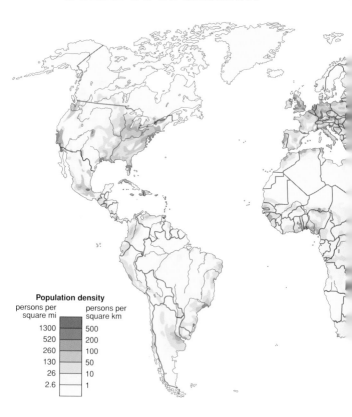

Population density

persons per square mi	persons per square km
1300	500
520	200
260	100
130	50
26	10
2.6	1

The world's population is very unevenly distributed across the globe. Mostly this is due to climatic conditions — vast areas of land including the Sahara in North Africa, the interior of Australia, Siberia, and the Amazon basin are inhospitable to human habitation. In the last century the population grew most quickly in nations that were industrializing — western Europe, and the northeastern United States; more population explosions are occurring

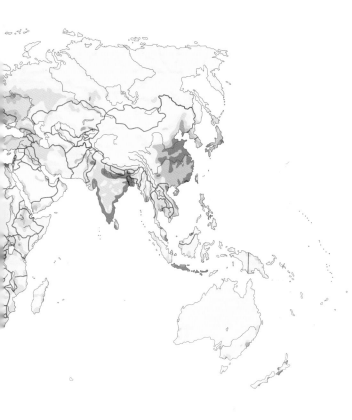

in developing countries, most notably India, China and Southeast Asia. In the 1990s about half of the world's population is living on 5 percent of the land area, and about half of the world's land area is home to only 5 percent of the population. Population pressure brings an increased demand for food, which in turn leads to the destruction of natural habitats, while crowded urban living has contributed to mounting environmental problems.

THE WORLD'S CLIMATE

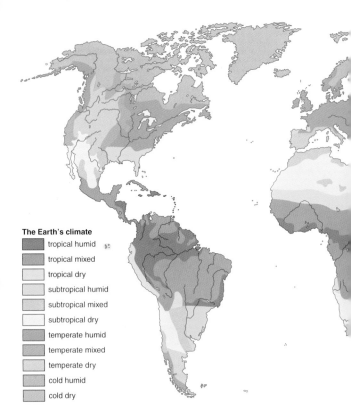

The Earth's climate

- tropical humid
- tropical mixed
- tropical dry
- subtropical humid
- subtropical mixed
- subtropical dry
- temperate humid
- temperate mixed
- temperate dry
- cold humid
- cold dry

The single most important factor affecting climate is latitude. Moving away from the equator the broad climatic bands change from tropical to subtropical to temperate to cold. In addition, the prevailing winds, topography, distance from the sea and sea currents affect rainfall and air temperature. Winds blowing off the sea tend to be moist, but when moist winds blow over a mountain range they cool as they rise, lose their capacity to hold water

18

and drop it as rain as they climb. As the winds blow down the other side of the mountain they grow warmer and collect moisture from the land, creating a dry region called a rain shadow. Ocean currents exert a huge influence over the land mass they surround. The British Isles and Newfoundland, Canada, share the same latitude, but Britain is heated by the warm Gulf stream, and Newfoundland is chilled by the cold Labrador Current.

Key to International Organizations

AfDB African Development Bank;
50 members

AL Arab League; 22 members

ANZUS Australia–New Zealand–United
States Security Treaty

APEC Asia–Pacific Economic
Cooperation; 18 members

ASEAN Association of South East Asian
Nations; 6 members

BCIE Central American Bank for
Economic Integration; 5 members

BDEAC Central African States
Development Bank; 9 members

BSEC Black Sea Economic Cooperation
Zone; 11 members

CACM Central American Common Market;
6 members

CARICOM Caribbean Community and
Common Market; 14 members

CBSS Council of the Baltic Sea States;
10 members

CIS Commonwealth of Independent
States; 10 members

CSCE Conference on Security and
Cooperation in Europe; 52 members

EBRD European Bank for Reconstruction
and Development; 59 members

ECA Economic Commission for Africa;
52 members

ECLAC Economic Commission for Latin
America and the Caribbean; 41 members

EFTA European Free Trade Association;
4 members

ESCAP Economic and Social Commission
for Asia and the Pacific; 46 members

EU European Union; 15 members

G-7 Group of Seven (major western powers)

GATT General Agreement on Tariffs and
Trade; 104 members

IAEA International Atomic Energy
Authority; 121 members

IBRD International Bank for
Reconstruction and Development (the
World Bank); 177 members

IDA International Development
Association; 177 members

IDB Islamic Development Bank;
45 members

IMF International Monetary Fund;
179 members

INTERPOL International Criminal Police;
146 members

LAES Latin American Economic System;
26 members

LAIA Latin American Integration
Association; 11 members

LORCS League of Red Cross and Red
Crescent Societies

NAM Non-aligned movement;
103 members

NATO North Atlantic Treaty Organization;
16 members

OAPEC Organization of Arab Petroleum-
Exporting countries; 11 members

OAU Organization of African Unity;
53 members

OECD Organization for Economic
Cooperation and Development; 25 members

OIC Organization of the Islamic
Conference; 48 members

OPEC Organization of Petroleum-
Exporting Countries; 12 members

UN United Nations; 184 members

UNCTAD United Nations Conference on
Trade and Development; 184 members

UNESCO United Nations Educational,
Scientific and Cultural Organization;
179 members

UNHCR United Nations High Commission
for Refugees; 46 members

UNPROFOR United Nations Protection
Force; 32 members

WHO World Health Organization;
189 members

NOTE Major Physical Features: longest river
The full length of the river is always given in
each data panel, though only part of the river
may run through that country.

A-Z OF
COUNTRIES
OF THE
WORLD

AFGHANISTAN

Land area 652,225 sq km (251,825 sq mi)	**Official religion** Islam
Major physical features highest point: Mount Nowshak 7,485 m (24,556 ft); longest river: Helmand (part) 1,400 km (870 mi)	**Religious affiliations** Sunni Muslim 84.0%; Shi'ite Muslim 15.0%; others 1.0%
Population (1994) 16,903,400	**Currency** 1 afghani (Af) = 100 puls
Form of government multiparty republic with two legislative houses (in a state of flux)	**Economy** Gross national product (per capita 1991) US $450
Largest cities Kabul (capital – 1,424,000); Kandahar (226,000); Herat (177,000)	**Life expectancy at birth** male 45.0 yr; female 44.0 yr
Official languages Pashto, Dari Persian	**Major resources** wheat, livestock, fruit, wool, natural gas, oil, coal, copper
Ethnic composition Pashtun 38.0%; Tajik 25.0%; Uzbek 6.0%; Hazara 19.0%; others 12.0%	**Major international organizations** ESCAP, IAEA, IMF, UN, UNESCO, WHO

Afghanistan is a land-locked state in the mountains of south-central Asia, bordering Pakistan to the southeast, Iran to the west, and the southwestern republics of the former Soviet Union to the north. It also controls the great land route to India via the Khyber Pass. Since the late 1970s Afghanistan has been torn by civil war, when a large group of Islamic fundamentalists began to wage a guerrilla campaign against the ruling communist regime, backed by the Soviets. In 1992 the Islamic forces gained control of the country, but fighting has persisted between various rebel factions. War and political instability have severely retarded the country's economic growth, and it remains one of the poorest in the world, depending on agriculture as the mainstay of the economy.

ALBANIA

Land area 28,748 sq km (11,100 sq mi)
Major physical features highest point:
Mount Korabit 2,751 m (9,026 ft); longest
river: Drin (part) 282 km (175 mi); largest
lake: Lake Scutari (part) 370 sq km (143 sq mi)
Population (1994) 3,374,085
Form of government multiparty republic
Largest cities Tiranë (capital – 243,000);
Durrës (79,000); Shkodër (76,000); Vlorë
(68,000)
Official language Albanian
Ethnic composition Albanian 95.0%; Greek
3.0%; others 2.0%

Religious affiliations Muslim 70.0%; Greek
Orthodox 20%; Roman Catholic 10%
Currency 1 lek (Lk) = 100 qintars
Economy Gross national product (per capita
1993) US $340; Gross domestic product
(1993) US $692 million
Life expectancy at birth (1994 est.) male
70.0 yr; female 77.0 yr
Major resources petroleum, natural gas,
coal, chromium, copper, timber, nickel
Major international organizations BSEC,
CSCE, EBRD, IAEA, IBRD, IDA, IDB, IMF,
INTERPOL, OIC, UN, UNESCO, WHO

Albania is a mountainous and primarily rural country in eastern Europe bordered by the
rump state of Yugoslavia to the north and northeast, Macedonia to the east, and Greece
to the southeast. Its inaccessible swamps and mountains have isolated Albania politically and economically from its neighbors and its hard-line communist government was the
last in Europe to give way to pressure for reform in the early 1990s. The collapse of the
communist regime, and subsequent economic slump, was closely followed by waves of
Muslim refugees fleeing from the war in former Yugoslavia, and food shortages are widespread. Albania lacks the infrastructure to promote growth of a market economy.

ALGERIA

Land area 2,381,741 sq km (919,595 sq mi)
Major physical features highest point: Mount Tahat 2,918 m (9,573 ft)
Population (1994) 27,895,068
Form of government multiparty republic
Largest cities Algiers (capital – 1,722,000); Oran (664,000); Constantine (449,000)
Official language Arabic
Ethnic composition Arab-Berber 99.0%; European less than 1%
Religious affiliations Sunni Muslim 99.0%; Christian and Jewish 1.0%

Currency 1 Algerian dinar = 100 centimes
Economy Gross national product (per capita 1993) US $1,780; Gross domestic product (1993) US $39,836 million
Life expectancy at birth male 66.6 yr; female 68.7 yr
Major resources petroleum, natural gas, iron ore, lead, coal, cork oak, wheat
Major international organizations AL, IMF, INTERPOL, OPEC, UN, UNESCO, UNHCR, WHO

Algeria, a former French colony, is the second largest country in Africa. In recent years the economy has mushroomed thanks to substantial deposits of natural gas and oil.

ANDORRA

Land area 468 sq km (181 sq mi)
Major physical feature highest point: Coma
Pedrosa 2,946 m (9,665 ft)
Population (1994) 63,930
Form of government (since March 1993)
Parliamentary democracy
Capital city Andorra la Vella (20,000)
Official language Catalan
Ethnic composition Spanish 61.0%;
Andorran 30.0%; French 6.0%; others 3.0%
Official religion Roman Catholicism

Religious affiliations Roman Catholic
94.2%; Jewish 0.4%; Jehovah's Witnesses 0.3%;
Protestant 0.2%; others 4.9%
Currency 1 French franc (F) = 100 cen-
times; 1 Spanish peseta (Pta) = 100 céntimos
Life expectancy at birth male 75.5 yr;
female 81.5 yr
Major resources Tourism
Major international organizations INTER-
POL, UN

Andorra is a tiny principality in the eastern Pyrenees, bordered by France to the north
and Spain to the south. The joint heads of state are the President of France and the
Bishop of Urgel, though real power lies in the hands of elected delegates and judges.
Andorra depends entirely on France and Spain for defense, a communications network,
and its education system. French and Spanish currencies coexist as legal tender, and
both languages are widely spoken, though Catalan predominates. The high mountainous
landscape means that scope for commercial agriculture is very limited, but in recent
years Andorra has taken advantage of its alpine scenery and cold winter climate to promote a tourist industry focused on winter skiing. Advantageous tax and custom laws
have also contributed to the growth of international commerce.

ANGOLA

Land area 1,246,700 sq km (481,354 sq mi)
Major physical feature highest point:
Mount Moco 2,610 m (8,563 ft)
Population (1994) 9,803,576
Form of government one-party republic
with one legislative house
Capital city Luanda (1,544,000)
Official language Portuguese
Ethnic composition Ovimbundu 37.0%;
Kimbundi 25.0%; Bakongo 13.0%; Mestico
(mixed European and African) 2.0%;
European 1.0%; others 22.0%

Religious affiliations indigenous beliefs
47.0%; Roman Catholic 38.0%; Protestant
15.0%
Currency 1 new kwanza (NKz) = 100 lwei
Economy Gross national product (per capita
1991) US $620
Life expectancy at birth male 43.7 yr;
female 47.9 yr
Major resources diamonds, gold, petroleum,
natural gas, iron ore, food crops, textiles
Major international organizations IMF,
INTERPOL, UN, UNESCO, WHO

Angola is a large state on the southwestern coast of Africa, bordered by Zaire to the
north, Zambia to the east and Namibia to the south. The northern enclave of Cabinda is
also Angolan territory. Bitter political warfare has destabilized the economy, but Angola's
rich natural resources, notably diamonds, gold and oil, offer potential prosperity.

ANTIGUA & BARBUDA

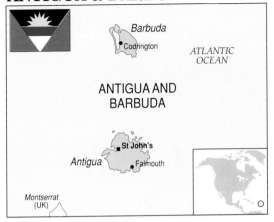

Land area 442 sq km (171 sq mi)
Major physical features highest point: Boggy Peak 405 m (1,329 ft); largest island: Antigua 280 sq km (108 sq mi)
Population (1994) 64,762
Form of government multiparty constitutional monarchy with two legislative houses
Capital city St. John's (36,000)
Official language English
Ethnic composition black 94.4%; mulatto 3.5%; white 1.3%; others 0.8%
Religious affiliations Anglican 44.5%; other

Protestants 41.6%; Roman Catholic 10.2%; Rastafarian 0.7%; others 3.0%
Currency 1 East Caribbean dollar (EC$) = 100 cents
Economy Gross national product (per capita 1991) US $4,770
Life expectancy at birth male 71.0 yr; female 75.0 yr
Major resources tourism
Major international organizations CARICOM, GATT, IBRD, IMF, INTERPOL, LORCS, UN, UNESCO, WHO

The two small islands that make up this nation are part of the Leeward Islands group. They were discovered by Christopher Columbus in 1493, colonized by Britain in the 1600s and achieved full independence in 1981. Their greatest assets are numerous white, sandy, palm-fringed beaches attracting thousands of foreign visitors. There are a number of casinos, popular with tourist clientele, and some fine 18th-century architecture in the capital, St. John's. Tourism accounts for most of the islands' revenue, indirectly feeding the other service industries including construction and communications. The location of the islands is of considerable strategic importance to the United States which has two military bases there.

ARGENTINA

Land area 2,780,092 sq km (1,073,399 sq mi)
Major physical features highest point: Aconcagua 6,960 m (22,834 ft); longest river: Paraná (part) 4,500 km (2,800 mi)
Population (1994) 33,912,994
Form of government federal multiparty republic with two legislative houses
Largest cities Buenos Aires (capital – 11,256,000); Córdoba (1,198,000)
Official language Spanish
Ethnic composition European 85.0%; mestizo/Amerindian 15.0%
Religious affiliations Roman Catholic 90.0%; Protestant 2.0%; Jewish 2.0%; others 6.0%
Currency 1 nuevo peso = 100 centavos
Economy Gross national product (per capita 1993) US $7,220
Life expectancy at birth male 68.0 yr; female 74.8 yr
Major resources meat, wheat, hides, wool
Major international organizations GATT, IMF, INTERPOL, LAIA, UN, UNESCO, WHO

Argentina is a long narrow state on the southern tip of South America. Although rich in natural resources, its development has been hampered by long-term political unrest.

ARMENIA

Land area 29,800 sq km (11,500 sq mi)
Major physical features highest point: Aragats 4,090 m (13,418 ft); longest river: Aras (part) 914 km (568 mi); largest lake: Lake Sevan 1,417 sq km (547 sq mi)
Population (1994) 3,521,517
Form of government multiparty republic with one legislative house
Largest cities Yerevan (capital – 1,202,000); Kirovakan (159,000); Kumayri (123,000)
Official language Armenian
Ethnic composition Armenian 93.0%; Azeri 3.0%; Russian 2.0%; others 2.0%
Religious affiliations Armenian Orthodox, with Catholic and Muslim minorities
Currency (since 1993) 1 dram = 100 luma
Economy Gross national product (per capita 1993) US $660; Gross domestic product (1993) US $2,190 million
Life expectancy at birth male 68.65 yr; female 75.65 yr
Major resources agriculture
Major international organizations IMF, INTERPOL, UN, UNESCO, WHO

Armenia is a tiny, landlocked republic in the mountains south of the Caucasus. It also claims territorial rights over the Armenian-populated enclave of Nagorno-Karabakh that lies beyond its eastern frontier in neighboring Azerbaijan. In 1988 a devastating earthquake destroyed most of the country's infrastructure, and economic recovery continues to be severely impeded by long-term conflict with Azerbaijan, which has cut off Armenia's main fuel and food supplies.

29

AUSTRALIA

Land area 7,682,300 sq km (2,966,200 sq mi)
Major physical features highest point: Mount Kosciusko 2,230 m (7,316 ft); longest river: Murray–Darling 3,780 km (2,330 mi)
Population (1994) 18,077,419
Form of government federal multiparty parliamentary state with two legislative houses
Largest cities Sydney (3,657,000); Melbourne (3,081,000); Brisbane (1,302,000); Perth (1,193,000); Canberra (capital 310,000)
Ethnic composition Caucasian 95.0%; Asian 4.0%; Aboriginal and others 1.0%

Religious affiliations Roman Catholic 26.0%; Anglican 26.1%; other Christians 24.3%
Currency 1 Australian dollar = 100 cents
Economy Gross national product (per capita 1993) US $17,500; Gross domestic product (1993) US $289,390 million
Life expectancy at birth male 74.5 yr; female 80.1 yr
Major resources coal, iron ore, copper, silver uranium, diamonds, natural gas, petroleum
Major international organizations ANZUS, GATT, INTERPOL, OECD, UN, UNESCO, WHO

Australia is the world's largest island and sixth largest country. The population is concentrated on the eastern and southeastern coasts, with two thirds of citizens living in eight cities. About 80 percent of the land is outback, expanses of parched empty land, too dry to support crops. Sheep farming on huge sheep stations is the economic mainstay in this terrain, making Australia the world's largest wool producer. Children on these stations receive their education by television and two-way radio, and the Flying Doctor service provides healthcare to the most isolated households. Mineral resources are plentiful; coal is a major export and gold, uranium, iron ore, diamonds, opals and bauxite are all being exploited. In the 1990s Australia is also encouraging the growth of newer industries such as tourism and telecommunications.

States and Territories
(with population for 1993)

Australian Capital Territory	(299,400)	**South Australia**	(1,466,500)
New South Wales	(6,023,500)	**Tasmania**	(472,100)
Northern Territory	(170,500)	**Victoria**	(4,468,300)
Queensland	(3,155,400)	**Western Australia**	(1,687,300)

AUSTRIA

Land area 83,857 sq km (32,377 sq mi)
Major physical features highest point:
Grossglockner 3,798 m (12,461 ft); longest
rivers: Danube (part) 2,850 km (1,770 mi)
Population (1994) 7,954,974
Form of government federal multiparty
republic with two legislative houses
Largest cities Vienna (capital – 1,540,000);
Linz (203,000); Graz (238,000); Salzburg
(144,000); Innsbruck (118,000)
Official language German
Ethnic composition Austrian 96.1%; Yugoslav
1.7%; Turkish 0.8%; German 0.5%; others 0.9%

Religious affiliations Roman Catholic
85.0%; Protestant 6.0%; others 9.0%
Currency 1 Schilling (S) = 100 Groschen
Economy Gross national product (per capita
1993) US $23,510; Gross domestic product
(1993) US $182,067 million
Life expectancy at birth male 73.4 yr;
female 80.0 yr
Major resources iron ore, timber, coal,
hydropower, copper, aluminium, petroleum
Major international organizations EU,
GATT, IMF, OECD, UN, UNESCO, UNHCR,
WHO

Austria is a mountainous land-locked state at the heart of Europe, bordering seven other
countries — the Czech Republic, Slovakia, Hungary, Solvenia, Germany, Switzerland and
Italy. This central position has given the country an important trading role, and during
the 20th century Austria has used its strategic advantage to transform its agricultural
economy to a modern industrial one. The magnificent alpine scenery makes it a major
tourist destination, particularly for winter skiing.

AZERBAIJAN

Land area 86,600 sq km (33,400 sq mi)
Major physical features highest point:
Bazar-Dyuzi 4,480 m (14,698 ft); lowest point:
Caspian Sea –28 m (–92 ft); longest river:
Kura (part) 1,510 km (940 mi)
Population (1994) 7,684,456
Form of government multiparty republic
Largest cities Baku (capital – 1,149,000);
Gyandzha (281,000); Sumgait (235,000)
Official language Azeri
Ethnic composition Azeri 82.0%; Russian
7.0%; Armenian 5.0%; others 6.0%

Religious affiliations Shi'ite Muslim, with
Sunni Muslim and Armenian Christian minorities
Currency 1 ruble (Rub) = 100 kopecks
Economy Gross national product (per capita
1993) US $730; Gross domestic product
(1993) US $4,992 million
Life expectancy at birth male 67.0 yr;
female 74.8 yr
Major resources petroleum, natural gas, iron
ore, other metal ores, agriculture, fishing
Major international organizations CIS, IMF,
INTERPOL, UN, UNESCO, WHO

Azerbaijan, a southeastern republic of the former Soviet Union, is extremely rich in
energy resources, but its potential prosperity is hampered by chronic territorial disputes
with neighboring Armenia over the enclaves of Nagorno-Karabakh and Nakhichevan.

BAHAMAS

Land area 13,939 sq km (5,382 sq mi)
Major physical features highest point: Cat island 63 m (206 ft); largest island: Andros 5,957 sq km (2,300 sq mi)
Population (1994) 273,005
Form of government multiparty constitutional monarchy with two legislative houses
Capital city Nassau (135,000)
Official language English
Ethnic composition black 72.3%; mixed 14.2%; white 12.9%; others 0.6%

Religious affiliations Baptist 32.1%; Anglican 20.1%; Roman Catholic 18.8%; Methodist 6.1%; other Christians 17.0%; others 5.9%
Currency 1 Bahamian dollar = 100 cents
Economy Gross national product (per capita 1991) US $11,720
Life expectancy at birth male 67.0 yr; female 74.0 yr
Major resources tourism, salt, timber
Major international organizations CARICOM, IMF, INTERPOL, UN, UNESCO, WHO

The Bahamas is the collective name for some 700 islands and reefs forming a long archipelago in the Caribbean southeast of Florida, in the United States, and north of Cuba. Most of the islands are fringed with picturesque mangroves, lagoons, coral reefs and golden beaches, and the larger islands are forested with Caribbean pine. The islands' natural beauty and their enormous variety of wildlife is their main resource, attracting thousands of tourists. The only mineral produced for export in significant quantities is salt. Until 1973 the Bahamas was a British colony, and the government is still run along British lines with the British monarch as the head of state, represented on the islands by a governor-general.

BAHRAIN

Land area 691 sq km (267 sq mi)
Major physical features largest island: Bahrain 583 sq km (225 sq mi); highest point: Dukhan Hill 134 m (440 ft)
Population (1994) 585,683
Form of government monarchy with one appointed council
Capital city Al Manamah (152,000)
Official language Arabic
Ethnic composition Bahraini 63.0%; Asian 13.0%; other Arab 10.0%; Iranian 8.0%; others 6.0%

Official religion Islam
Religious affiliations Shi'ite Muslim 70.0%; Sunni Muslim 30.0%
Currency 1 Bahraini dinar (BD) = 1,000 fils
Economy Gross national product (per capita 1991) US $6,910
Life expectancy at birth male 71.7 yr; female 76.0 yr
Major resources petroleum, aluminum, natural gas, fishing
Major international organizations GATT, IMF, INTERPOL, OAPEC, UN, UNESCO, WHO

Bahrain is an independent monarchy consisting of some 30 islands in the Gulf of Bahrain, a small branch of the Persian Gulf between Saudi Arabia and Qatar. The landscape is low-lying and arid, but underground springs and desalination plants have enabled Bahrain to be almost self-sufficient in fruit and vegetables. Rich deposits of petroleum and natural gas have made Bahrain prosperous, but in the mid-1990s reserves are dwindling. The aluminum-processing industry and the newly developed financial services sector seem likely to take over as major revenue-earners.

BANGLADESH

Land area 143,998 sq km (55,598 sq mi)
Major physical feature longest river:
Brahmaputra (part) 2,900 km (1,800 mi)
Population (1994) 125,149,469
Form of government multiparty republic
Largest cities Dhaka (capital – 6,105,000);
Chittagong (2,041,000); Khulna (877,000);
Rajshahi (517,000); Narayanganj (406,000)
Official language Bangla (Bengali)
Ethnic composition Bengali 97.7%; Bihari
1.3%; others 1.0%
Official religion Islam

Religious affiliations Muslim 83%; Hindu
16%; Buddhist 0.6%; Christian 0.3%; others 0.4%
Currency 1 Bangladesh taka = 100 paisa
Economy Gross national product (per capita
1993) US $22; Gross domestic product (1993)
US $23,977 million
Life expectancy at birth male 55.3 yr;
female 54.8 yr
Major resources jute, cotton
Major international organizations ESCAP,
GATT, IMF, OIC, UN, UNPROFOR, WHO

Bangladesh, literally "land of the Bengalis", is in the northeastern corner of the Indian
subcontinent and occupies the eastern two-thirds of the Ganges-Brahmaputra delta,
where it flows into the Bay of Bengal. Bangladesh is one of the poorest, most densely
populated and least developed countries in the world. The economy is overwhelmingly
agricultural, but frequent cyclones and floods prevent the growth of this sector and
contribute to regional food shortages. Industrialization is at a very low level.

BARBADOS

Land area 430 sq km (166 sq mi)
Major physical feature highest point: Mount Hillaby 336 m (1,102 ft)
Population (1994) 255,827
Form of government multiparty constitutional monarchy with two legislative houses
Capital city Bridgetown (7,000)
Official language English
Ethnic composition black 91.9%; white 3.3%; mulatto 2.6%; Indian 0.5%; others 1.7%
Religious affiliations Anglican 39.7%; other Protestants 25.6%; nonreligious 20.2%; Roman Catholic 4.4%; others 10.1%
Currency 1 Barbadan dollar = 100 cents
Economy Gross national product (per capita 1993) US $5,700
Life expectancy at birth male 71.7 yr; female 76.8 yr
Major resources sugar, cotton, tourism
Major international organizations CARICOM, GATT, UN, IBRD, IMF, NAM, UN, UNESCO, WHO

Barbados is an island state in the Caribbean, lying outside the Lesser Antilles some 375 km (233 mi) off the northeast coast of Venezuela. It was settled by the British in 1627, who developed sugar plantations to supply their domestic market. It became a fully independent member of the British Commonwealth in 1966, but still retains aspects of British cultural life. Present-day Barbadans are descended from slaves, liberated in the 1830s. Agriculture continues to be dominated by sugar cane production (with small-scale processing industries exporting its byproducts, molasses and rum) but diversification into other crops such as citrus fruits and cotton is on the increase. Tourism is the single largest contributor to the economy, creating in Barbados one of the highest standards of living of all the eastern Caribbean island states.

BELARUS

Land area 207,600 sq km (80,200 sq mi)
Major physical features highest point: Dzerzhinsky 346 m (1,135 ft); longest river: Dnieper (part) 2,280 km (1,420 mi)
Population (1994) 10,404,862
Form of government multiparty republic
Largest cities Minsk (capital – 1,613,000); Gomel (506,000); Mogilev (363,000)
Ethnic composition Belarus 77.9%; Russian 13.2%; Polish 4.1%; Ukrainian 2.1%; others 2.7%
Official language Belorussian

Religious affiliations Orthodox & Catholic
Currency 1 ruble (Rub) = 100 kopecks
Economy Gross national product (per capita 1993) US $2,870; Gross domestic product (1993) US $27,545 million
Life expectancy at birth male 66.2 yr; female 75.8 yr
Major resources coal, petroleum, metal ores, salt, dairy products, meat, grain, sugar
Major international organizations CIS, IBRD, IMF, UN, UNESCO, WHO

The former Soviet republic of Belarus lies between Poland and the Russian Federation. It is one of the most developed industrial and agricultural economies in the region.

38

BELGIUM

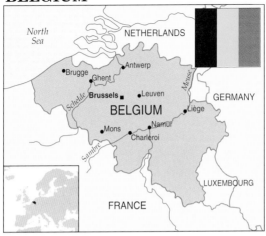

Land area 30,518 sq km (11,783 sq mi)
Major physical features highest point: Botrange 694 m (2,276 ft); longest rivers: Meuse (part) 930 km (580 mi) and Schelde 435 km (270 mi)
Population (1994) 10,062,836
Form of government multiparty constitutional monarchy with two legislative houses
Largest cities Brussels (capital – 1,331,000); Antwerp (668,000); Ghent (251,000)
Official languages Dutch, French, German
Ethnic composition Flemish/Walloon 91.1%; Italian 2.8%; Moroccan 1.1%; French 1.1%; Dutch 0.7%; Turkish 0.6%; others 2.6%

Religious affiliations Roman Catholic 90.0%; Muslim 1.1%; Protestant 0.4%; nonreligious 7.5%; others 1.0%
Currency 1 Belgian franc = 100 centimes
Economy Gross national product (per capita 1993) US $21,650; Gross domestic product (1993) US $25,242 million
Life expectancy at birth male 73.7 yr; female 80.4 yr
Major resources Belgium imports raw materials and exports manufactured goods
Major International organizations EU, GATT, IMF, INTERPOL, NATO, OECD, UN, UNESCO, UNPROFOR, WHO

Belgium lies on the North Sea coast of Europe, with the Netherlands to the northeast, Germany to the east, the Grand Duchy of Luxembourg to the southeast, and France to the south and west. The Belgians are made up of two distinct groups. More than half the population, concentrated in the North, are Flemish, and speak a dialect of Dutch. The remainder, concentrated in the south, are French-speaking Walloons. Although forced to import most raw materials, Belgium has built up an enormous variety of specialist manufacturing industries, making it one of Europe's most important commercial centers.

39

BELIZE

Land area 22,965 sq km (8,867 sq mi)
Major physical feature highest point: Victoria Peak 1,122 m (3,681 ft)
Population (1994) 208,949
Form of government multiparty constitutional monarchy with two legislative houses
Largest cities Belize City (40,000); Orange Walk (8,440); Dangriga (6,627); Belmopan (capital – 5,000)
Official language English
Ethnic composition Mestizo 44.0%; Creole 30.0%; Manja 11.0%; Garifuna 7.0%; other 8.0%

Religious affiliations Roman Catholic 61.7%; Protestant 28.9%; Baha'i 2.5%; Jewish 1.2%; other Christians 1.0%; others 4.7%
Currency 1 Belize dollar (Bz$) = 100 cents
Economy Gross national product (per capita 1991) US $2,050
Life expectancy at birth male 66.1 yr; female 70.1 yr
Major resources sugar, fruit crops, tourism, timber
Major international organizations CARICOM, GATT, IBRD, IMF, LAES, UN, WHO

Belize, formerly known as British Honduras, is a small country on the Caribbean coast of Central America, bordered by Mexico to the north and Guatemala to the west. It became independent from Britain in 1981, but remains within the Commonwealth and has a parliamentary government run along British lines. The economy is mainly agricultural, and sugar cane is the main crop, followed by citrus fruits. The main exports are refined sugar (40% of export revenue), rum, hardwoods, and citrus products. Most of the population is Catholic, and many of the state-funded schools are run by the church.

BENIN

Land area 112,600 sq km (43,450 sq mi)
Major physical feature highest point: Atakora Massif 641 m (2,103 ft)
Population (1994) 5,341,710
Form of government multiparty republic with one legislative house
Largest cities Cotonou (487,000); Porto-Novo (capital – 208,000); Parakou (66,000)
Official language French
Ethnic composition Fon 65.6%; Bariba 9.7%; Yoruba 8.9%; Somba 5.4%; Fulani 4.0%; others 6.4%

Religious affiliations indigenous beliefs 70.0%; Muslim 15.0%; Christian 15.0%
Currency 1 CFA franc = 100 centimes
Economy Gross national product (per capita 1993) US $430; Gross domestic product (1993) US $2,125 million
Life expectancy at birth male 49.9 yr; female 53.7 yr
Major resources oil, cotton, palm products, cocoa, coffee, gold
Major international organizations ECA, GATT, IMF, INTERPOL, UN, UNESCO, WHO

Benin (formally the French colony Dahomey) is a republic on the west coast of Africa, bordered by Togo to the west, Burkina Faso and Niger to the north, and Nigeria to the east. Over half the population is dependent on agriculture; living conditions are poor.

BHUTAN

Land area 47,000 sq km (18,150 sq mi)

Major physical feature highest point: Kula Kangri 7,554 m (24,783 ft)

Population (1994) 716,380

Form of government nonparty constitutional monarchy with one legislative house

Capital city Thimphu (27,000)

Official language Dzongkha (a form of Tibetan)

Ethnic composition Bhote 50.0%; Nepalese 35.0%; indigenous or migrant tribes 15.0%

Official religion Mahayana Buddhism

Religious affiliations Buddhist 69.6%; Hindu 24.6%; Muslim 5.0%; others 0.8%

Currency 1 ngultrum (Nu) = 100 chetrum

Economy Gross national product (per capita 1993) US $180

Life expectancy at birth male 51.5 yr; female 50.0 yr

Major resources timber, cardamon and other spices, gemstones, hydropower, gypsum, calcium carbide

Major international organizations IBRD, IMF, NAM, UN, UNESCO, UNIDO, WHO

Bhutan is a tiny isolated kingdom in the eastern Himalayas, out of the main stream of politics and commerce and regarded by the rest of the world as a secret and mysterious place. The Dragon King is the absolute ruler, presiding over an isolationist society where tourists are banned, except in escorted groups, and where people are forbidden by law to watch foreign or satellite television. The climate ranges from subtropical in the south to alpine in the north, but most of the population lives in the central temperate valleys where there is seasonal pastureland. Agriculture is the mainstay of the economy, and almost all trade is with India, where Bhutan exports hydropower, spices and gemstones.

BOLIVIA

Land area 1,098,581 sq km (424,164 sq mi)
Major physical features highest point:
Sajama 6,542 m (21,463 ft); largest lake: Lake
Titicaca (part) 8,340 sq km (3,220 sq mi)
Population (1994) 7,719,445
Form of government multiparty republic
with two legislative houses
Largest cities La Paz (administrative capi-
tal, 1,126,000); Santa Cruz (696,000);
Cochabamba (413,000); Oruro (208,000);
Sucre (judicial capital – 101,000)
Official languages Spanish, Quechua, Aymará
Ethnic composition Quechua 30.0%; Aymará
25.0%; mestizo (mixed European and Indian

descent) 25.0%–30.0%; European 5.0%–15.0%
Religious affiliations Roman Catholic
92.5%; Baha'i 2.6%; others 4.9%
Currency 1 boliviano (Bs) = 100 centavos
Economy Gross national product (per capita
1993) US $760; Gross domestic product
(1993) US $5,382 million
Life expectancy at birth male 60.9 yr;
female 65.9 yr
Major resources metal ores (tin, tungsten,
zinc) natural gas, coffee, sugar, timber, cotton
Major international organizations GATT,
IBRD, IMF, INTERPOL, LAES, LAIA, UN,
UNESCO, WHO

Bolivia is a landlocked state in central South America. Most of the population lives on
the Altiplano, a plateau between two ranges of the Andes, and over half of them are
dependent on agriculture for their living. Officially, coffee and sugar are the most important cash crops, but exporting illegal cocaine is also a major source of revenue.

BOSNIA HERZEGOVINA

Land area 51,129 sq km (19,741 sq mi)
Major physical features highest point:
Maglic 2,387 m (7,831 ft); longest rivers: Sava
(part) 940 km (584 mi), Bosna 241 km (150 mi)
Population (1994) 4,651,485*
Form of government not available
Largest cities Sarajevo (capital – 526,000);
Banja Luka (143,000)
Official language Serbo-Croat
Ethnic composition Muslim 44.0%; Serb
31.0%; Croat 17.0%; others 8.0%

Religious affiliations Muslims 40.0%;
Orthodox 31.0%; Catholic 15.0%; Protestant
4.0%; others 10.0%
Currency 1 dinar (Din) = 100 paras
Life expectancy at birth male 72.4 yr;
female 78.0 yr
Economy mainly agricultural, but with
extensive mineral resources. Industrialization
is limited and hampered by civil war

* subject to considerable error through military action
and ethnic cleansing

Bosnia Herzegovina came into existence in March 1992 following a referendum that
divided the former state of Yugoslavia into five republics. Interethnic civil war continues.

BOTSWANA

Land area 581,730 sq km (224,607 sq mi)
Major physical feature highest point: Tsodilo Hills 1,375 m (4,511 ft)
Population (1994) 1,359,352
Form of government multiparty republic with one legislative house
Capital city Gaborone (138,000)
Official language English
Ethnic composition Tswana 95%; Kalanga, Basarwa and Kgalagadi 4%; white 1%
Religious affiliations traditional beliefs 49.2%; Protestant 29.0%; African Christian 11.8%; Roman Catholic 9.4%; others 0.6%
Currency 1 pula (P) = 100 thebe
Economy Gross national product (per capita 1993) US $2,790; Gross domestic product (1993) US $3,813 million
Life expectancy at birth male 60.0 yr; female 66.2 yr
Major resources diamonds, copper, nickel, coal, salt, cattle farming, peanuts
Major international organizations GATT, IBRD, IMF, INTERPOL, UN, UNESCO, WHO

Botswana is a landlocked state in southern Africa, in customs union with its powerful neighbor, South Africa, on whom it depends for prosperity. Some 80% of the population still depends on cattle farming and agriculture for its livelihood, exporting meat and hides. Mining diamonds, copper and nickel is heavily subsidized by South Africa, and the government is developing an industrial sector. Tourism is beginning to grow.

BRAZIL

Land area 8,456,508 sq km (3,265,076 sq mi)
Major physical features highest point: Neblina Peak 3,014 m (9,888 ft); longest river: Amazon (part) 6,570 km (4,080 mi)
Population (1994) 158,739,257
Form of government federal multiparty republic with two legislative houses
Largest cities São Paulo (9,627,000); Rio de Janeiro (5,473,000); Belo Horizonte (2,017,000); Brasília (capital – 1,598,000)
Official language Portuguese
Ethnic composition mulatto 22.0%; Portuguese 15.0%; mestizo 12.0%; Italian 11.0%; black 11.0%; Spanish 10.0%; German 3.0%; other whites 14.0%; others 2.0%
Religious affiliations Roman Catholic 63.1%; Spiritist Catholic 15.7%; Evangelical Catholic 9.0%; Protestant 6.1%; Spiritist 3.7%; nonreligious 1.4%; others 1.0%
Currency 1 cruzeiro real = 100 centavos
Economy Gross national product (per capita 1993) US $2,930; Gross domestic product (1993) US $444,205 million
Life expectancy at birth male 57.4 yr; female 67.3 yr
Major resources gold, diamonds, coffee, iron
Major international organizations GATT, ECLAC, IMF, LAES, LAIA, UN, WHO

Brazil is the largest country in South America and its vast Amazon river basin contains the most extensive river system in the world. Despite problems in the early 1990s with debt and hyperinflation, Brazil's rich natural resources offer potential prosperity.

46

States of the Republic (with population for 1991)

NORTH		Ceará	(6,353,346)	Rio de Janeiro	(12,584,108)
Acre	(417,437)	Maranhão	(4,922,339)	São Paulo	(31,192,818)
Amapá	(289,050)	Paraíba	(3,200,620)	**SOUTH**	
Amazonas	(2,088,682)	Pernambuco	(7,109,626)	**Parana**	(8,415,659)
Rondônia	(1,130,400)	Piauí	(2,581,054)	**Rio Grande do Sul**	(9,127,611)
Roraima	(215,790)	Rio Grande do Norte		Santa Catarina	(4,536,433)
Pará	(5,084,726)		(2,413,618)	**CENTRAL WEST**	
Tocantins	(920,133)	Sergipe	(1,492,400)	**Federal District**	(1,596,274)
NORTH-EAST		**SOUTH-EAST**		Goiás	(4,024,547)
Alagoas	(2,512,515)	Espírito Santo	(2,598,231)	Mato Grosso	(2,020,581)
Bahia	(11,801,810)	Minas Gerais	(15,746,200)	Mato Grosso do Sul	(1,778,494)

BRUNEI

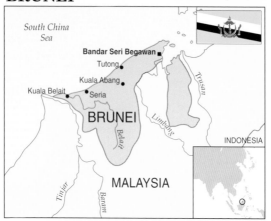

Land area   5,765 sq km (2,226 sq mi)
Major physical feature   highest point: Pagonprick 1,850 m (6,070 ft)
Population   (1994) 284,653
Form of government   nonparty constitutional monarchy with one advisory body
Capital city   Bandar Seri Begawan (46,000)
Official language   Malay
Ethnic composition   Malay 64.0%; Chinese 20.0%; others 16.0%
Official religion   Islam

Religious affiliations   Muslim 63.0%; Buddhist 14.0%; Christian 8.0%; others 15.0%
Currency   1 Brunei dollar (B$) = 100 cents
Economy   Gross national product (per capita 1991) US $6,000
Life expectancy at birth   male 69.5yr; female 72.8 yr
Major resources   petroleum, natural gas, hardwood, pepper, rice, cork, rubber
Major international organizations   APEC, GATT, NAM, UN, UNTAC, WHO

Brunei, officially the "Sultanate of Brunei, Abode of Peace", is an independent monarchy on the northwest coast of Borneo, surrounded and divided in two by the Malaysian state of Sarawak. The two parts of the country are separated by a few kilometers of coastline where the Limbang river enters Brunei Bay. Following Japanese occupation during World War II, Brunei reverted to British rule, becoming independent in 1984. It is the least densely populated country in Southeast Asia, and its more remote areas are a haven for wildlife. Most of the country is covered in tropical hardwood forests, sweeping down to a narrow and swampy coastal plain. Rich reserves of petroleum and natural gas have given Brunei one of the largest per-capita incomes in Southeast Asia, enabling the government to set up comprehensive free healthcare and a free education service. Its absolute ruler, the Sultan of Brunei, is one of the wealthiest individuals in the world.

BULGARIA

Land area 110,994 sq km (42,855 sq mi)
Major physical features highest point: Musala 2,925 m (9,594 ft); longest river: Danube (part) 2,850 km (1,770 mi)
Population (1994) 8,799,986
Form of government multiparty republic with one legislative house
Largest cities Sofia (capital – 1,141,000); Plovdiv (379,000); Varna (315,000)
Official language Bulgarian
Ethnic composition Bulgarian 85.3%; Turkish 8.5%; Gypsy 2.6%; Macedonian 2.5%; Armenian 0.3%; Russian 0.2%; others 0.6%

Religious affiliations Bulgarian Orthodox 85.0%; Muslim 13.0%; Jewish 0.8%; Roman Catholic 0.5%; Uniate Catholic 0.2%; others 0.5%
Currency 1 lev (Lv) = 100 stotinki
Economy Gross national product (per capita 1993) US $1,140; Gross domestic product (1993) US $10,369 million
Life expectancy at birth male 69.9 yr; female 76.7 yr
Major resources copper, iron ore, coal, tobacco, grapes (wine), fisheries
Major international organizations BSEC, IAEA, IMF, NAM, UN, UNESCO, WHO

Bulgaria lies on the eastern side of the Balkan peninsula. In former decades it was one of the most acquiescent of the Soviet satellite states, but since the "quiet revolution" of 1989 it has been transformed into a democratic state with a free-market economy. Manufacturing industry specializes in machinery, metal processing and petrochemicals.

BURKINA FASO

Land area 274,200 sq km (105,869 sq mi)
Major physical feature highest point: Tena Kourou 747 m (2,451 ft)
Population (1994) 10,134,661
Form of government parliamentary republic
Largest cities Ouagadougou (capital – 442,000); Bobo Dioulasso (231,000)
Official language French
Ethnic composition Mossi 47.9%; Mande 8.8%; Fulani 8.3%; Lobi 6.9%; Bobo 6.8%; Senufo 5.3%; Grosi 5.1%; Gurma 4.8%; Tuareg 3.3%; others 2.8%
Religious affiliations traditional beliefs 44.8%; Muslim 43.0%; Roman Catholic 9.8%; Protestant 2.4%
Currency 1 CFA franc = 100 centimes
Economy Gross national product (per capita 1993) $300; Gross domestic product (1993) US $2,698 million
Life expectancy at birth male 46.2 yr; female 47.9 yr
Major resources manganese, limestone, marble, antimony, copper, nickel, bauxite,
Major international organizations GATT, IMF, NAM, OIC, UN, UNESCO, WHO

Burkina Faso (known as Upper Volta until 1984) is a landlocked state on the southern fringe of the Sahara. The north is arid semi-desert, while the south is more tropical, though damaged in recent years by recurrent drought. It became independent of France in 1960, but government since then has been unstable, and rocked by frequent coups. The volatile political climate has hindered development. Most of the population is dependent on agriculture, and Burkina Faso is one of the poorest countries in the world.

BURUNDI

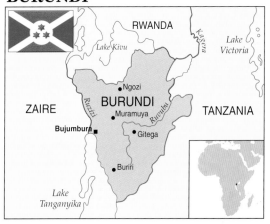

Land area 25,967 sq km (10,026 sq mi)
Major physical feature largest lake: Lake Tanganyika (part) 32,893 sq km (12,700 sq mi)
Population (1994) 6,124,747
Form of government republic with military government
Capital city Bujumbura (241,000)
Official languages Kirundi, French
Ethnic composition Hutu 85%; Tutsi 14%; Twa Pygmy 1.0%
Religious affiliations Christian 67%; indigenous beliefs 32%; Muslim 1%
Currency 1 Burundi franc = 100 centimes
Economy Gross national product (per capita 1993) US $180; Gross domestic product (1993) US $855 million
Life expectancy at birth male 38.3 yr; female 42.3 yr
Major resources coffee, cotton, nickel, uranium, rare earth oxide, peat, cobalt, copper
Major international organizations GATT, IMF, NAM, UN, UNESCO, WHO

Burundi is a small landlocked state in Central Africa, just south of the equator on the northeastern shores of Lake Tanganyika. To the north it shares a border with Rwanda, to whom it was formally federated. Originally the region was inhabited by a pygmy race, the Twa; later a people called the Hutu settled the area, but both groups were subjugated by the nomadic cattle-owning Tutsi. When Burundi was granted its independence from Germany in 1962, it was as a Tutsi kingdom; but the Hutu resisted Tutsi rule, organizing a series of coups. After one such coup in 1972 huge numbers of Hutu were massacred; in 1988 almost 3,000 families were wiped out and 60,000 people fled abroad. Unrest has destabilized the economy, which depends on subsistence farming, with some small-scale mining. Manufacturing industry is still in its infancy.

CAMBODIA

Land area 181,035 sq km (69,898 sq mi)
Major physical features highest point: Mount Aural 1,813 m (5,948 ft); longest river: Mekong (part) 4,180 km (2,600 mi); largest lake: Tonle Sap 10,000 sq km (3,860 sq mi)
Population (1994) 10,264,628
Form of government one-party republic with one legislative house
Capital city Phnom Penh (800,000)
Official language Khmer
Ethnic composition Khmer 90%; Vietnamese 5%; Chinese 1%; others 4%

Official religion Buddhism
Religious affiliations Buddhist 95%; others 5%
Currency 1 riel (C Rl) = 100 sen
Economy Gross national product (per capita 1991) US $200
Life expectancy at birth male 47.8 yr; female 50.8 yr
Major resources rice, fisheries, hardwood, rubber, gemstones
Major international organizations ESCAP, IAEA, IMF, NAM, UN, UNESCO, WHO

Cambodia is a lowland country in Indochina, bordering Vietnam to the east and the Gulf of Thailand to the west. It suffered considerably during the 1960s-70s from its involvement in the Vietnam war, when many Cambodians supported the Communist North Vietnamese against the United States. As a result, the country was subjected to carpet bombing by US forces 1970-73. Left-wing opinion is still fiercely strong in Cambodia, spearheaded by the *Khmer Rouge*, a radical group that seized power in 1975, prompting a long and bloody civil war in which over 2 million people died. Despite an uneasy truce introducing powersharing in 1991, Cambodia continues to experience instability.

CAMEROON

Land area 463,511 sq km (178,963 sq mi)
Major physical feature highest point: Mount Cameroon 4,070 m (13,353 ft)
Population (1994) 13,132,191
Form of government multiparty republic with one legislative house
Largest cities Douala (884,000); Yaoundé (capital – 750,000)
Official languages French, English
Ethnic composition Cameroon Highlanders 31%; Equatorial Bantu 19%; Kirdi 11%; Fulani 10%; Northwestern Bantu 8%; Eastern Nigritic 7%; other African 13%; non-African 1%

Religious affiliations indigenous beliefs 51%; Christian 33%; Muslim 16%
Currency 1 CFA franc = 100 centimes
Economy Gross national product (per capita 1993) US $820; Gross domestic product (1993) US $11,082 million
Life expectancy at birth male 55.0 yr; female 59.2 yr
Major resources petroleum, coffee, bananas, rubber, bauxite, iron ore, timber
Major international organizations GATT, IBRD, IMF, NAM, OIC, UN, UNESCO, WHO

Cameroon lies on the Gulf of Guinea on the west African coast. At the end of World War I the territory was divided between France and Britain. The country was not united until 1972. Since then, exploitation of Cameroon's oil reserves has boosted its prosperity.

CANADA

Land area 9,976,140 sq km (3,851,791 sq mi)
Major physical features longest river: Mackenzie 4,240 km (2,635 mi); largest lake Lake Superior (part) 83,270 sq km (32,150 sq mi)
Population (1994) 28,113,997
Form of government federal multiparty parliamentary monarchy, two legislative houses
Cities Toronto (3,893,000); Montreal (3,127,000); Ottawa (capital – 921,000)
Official languages English, French
Ethnic origin British 40.0%; French 27.0%; other European 20.0%; indigenous Indian and Innuit 1.5%; others 11.5%

Religious affiliations Roman Catholic 46.5%; Protestant 41.2%; Eastern Orthodox 1.5%; Jewish 1.2%; others 9.6%
Currency 1 Canadian dollar = 100 cents
Economy Gross national product (per capita 1993) US $19,970; Gross domestic product (1993) US $477,468 million
Life expectancy at birth male 74.7 yr; female 81.7 yr
Major resources petroleum, natural gas, coal, timber, wheat, nickel, zinc, copper, fisheries
Major international organizations ECLAC, G-7, GATT, IMF, NATO, UN, UNPROFOR, WHO

Canada occupies most of the northern half of the North American continent, though its population is concentrated near the southern border, alongside the United States. Its economy and culture closely resembles that of the US. Both are rich in minerals and agricultural resources, have a skilled labor force, modern industrial plant, free market economies, and have affluent highly developed industrial and urban economies.

Provinces and Territories

(with population for 1991)

Alberta	(2,545,553)	Nova Scotia	(899,942)
British Columbia	(3,282,061)	Ontario	(10,084,885)
Manitoba	(1,091,942)	Prince Edward Island	(129,765)
New Brunswick	(723,900)	Quebec	(6,895,953)
Newfoundland	(568,474)	Saskatchewan	(988,928)
Northwest Territories	(57,649)	Yukon Territory	(27,797)

N.B.   NEW BRUNSWICK
N.S.   NOVA SCOTIA
P.E.I.   PRINCE EDWARD ISLAND

CAPE VERDE

Land area 4,033 sq km (1,557 sq mi)
Major physical features highest point: Pico do Cano (Fogo) 2,829 m (9,281 ft); largest island: São Tiago 991 sq km (383 sq mi)
Population (1994) 428,120
Form of government multiparty republic with one legislative house
Capital city Praia (62,000)
Official language Portuguese
Ethnic composition Creole (mulatto) 71.0%; African 28.0%; European 1.0%

Religious affiliations Roman Catholic 97.8%; others 2.2%
Currency 1 escudo (CVEsc) = 100 centavos
Economy Gross national product (per capita 1991) US $750
Life expectancy at birth male 60.7 yr; female 64.6 yr
Major resources corn, coconuts, sugar cane, salt, basalt rock, pozzolana, limestone, fish
Major international organizations IMF, NAM, UN (a non-permanent seat since 1992)

Cape Verde is made up of two small archipelagos of islands 50 km (31 mi) off the coast of Senegal in western Africa. All the islands are volcanic, ringed by steep cliffs and reefs, and eroded into jagged shapes. The economy is based on agriculture and fishing, though periodic droughts have devastated crop yields. Salt and a volcanic rock used in cement are among the very sparse mineral resources; tourism is a growth industry.

CENTRAL AFRICAN REPUBLIC

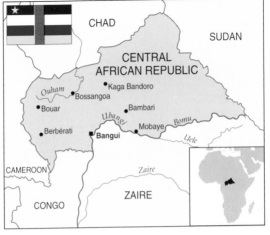

Land area   622,436 sq km (240,324 sq mi)
Major physical feature   highest point:
Kayagangiri 1,420 m (4,660 ft)
Population   (1994) 3,142,182
Form of government   one-party republic
with one legislative house
Capital city   Bangui (597,000)
Official language   French, Sango
Ethnic composition   Banja 34.0%; Banda
27.0%; Sara 10.0%; Mandjia 20.0%; Mboum
4.0%; M'Baka 4.0%; Europeans & others 1.0%
Religious affiliations   Protestant 25.0%;

Roman Catholic 25.0%; traditional beliefs
14.0%; Muslim 15.0%; others 21.0%
Currency   1 CFA franc = 100 centimes
Economy   Gross national product (per capita
1993) US $400; Gross domestic product
(1993) US $1,172 million
Life expectancy at birth   male 43.9 yr;
female 47.1 yr
Major resources   diamonds, uranium, timber,
gold, oil
Major international organizations BDAEC,
GATT, IMF, NAM, UN, UNESCO, WHO

Central African Republic is a landlocked country right in the heart of Africa. Most of the
territory is an undulating plateau flanked by mountains to the north and west, with the
climate ranging from near-desert in the north, to savanna grassland and open forest in
the center, to lush equatorial vegetation in the south. Slave traders in the 19th century
practically wiped out the indigenous pygmy peoples, and the area was resettled by
Bantu and Azande tribes. France colonized the country in 1911, naming it French
Congo, and it took the name Central African Republic on gaining full independence in
1958. After a period of military dictatorship, democratic elections were held in 1987.

CHAD

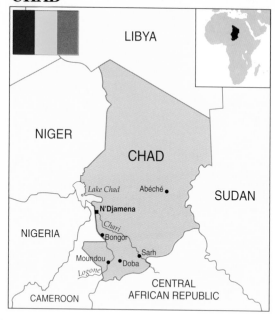

Land area 1,284,000 sq km (496,000 sq mi)
Major physical features highest point: Emi Koussi 3,415 m (11,204 ft); longest river: Chari 1,200 km (750 mi)
Population (1994) 5,466,771
Form of government one-party republic
Capital city N'Djamena (688,000)
Official languages Arabic, French
Ethnic composition Sara/Bagirmi/Kreish 30.5%; Sudanic Arab 26.1%; Teda 7.3%; Mbum 6.5%; Masalit/Maba/Mimi 6.3%; Tama 6.3%; Mubi 4.2%; Kanuri 2.3%; Hausa 2.3%; Masa 2.3%; Kotoko 2.1%; others 3.8%
Religious affiliations Sunni Muslim 50.0%; Christian 25.0%; traditional & others 25.0%
Currency 1 CFA franc = 100 centimes
Economy Gross national product (per capita 1993) US $210; Gross domestic product (1993) US $1,133 million
Life expectancy at birth male 39.7 yr; female 41.9 yr
Major resources petroleum (unexploited)
Major international organizations BDEAC, GATT, IMF, NAM, UN, UNESCO, WHO

The republic of Chad in central Africa straddles the drought-stricken area of the Sahel. Civil war and conflict with its neighbor Libya have severely hampered its development.

58

CHILE

Land area 756,626 sq km (292,135 sq mi)

Population (1994) 13,950,557

Form of government multiparty republic

Capital city Santiago (5,343,000)

Official language Spanish

Ethnic composition mestizo 91.6%; Amerindian 6.8%; others 1.6%

Religious affiliations Roman Catholic 80.7%; Protestant 6.1%; Jewish 0.2%; nonreligious 12.8%; others 0.2%

Currency 1 Chilean peso = 100 centavos

Economy Gross national product (per capita 1993) US $3,170; Gross domestic product (1993) US $43,684 million

Life expectancy at birth male 71.5 yr; female 77.6 yr

Major resources copper, timber, iron ore, precious metals, nitrates

Chile occupies a narrow mountainous strip of land along the southwestern coast of South America. It has rich natural resources and a thriving manufacturing sector.

CHINA

China is the third largest country in the world, occupying almost one quarter of the landmass of Asia, and sharing borders with 14 other countries. It is also the world's most populous nation, with over a billion citizens, accounting for almost one fifth of the total population of the world. China's enormous size allows it to encompass a huge variety of terrain and climate. They include the icy Himalayas and the plateau of Tibet in the south-west, a series of desert basins in the remote northeast and northwest on the borders of Mongolia, the densely populated lowlands of the north China plains, and the tropical southeast coast close to Hong Kong and Macao. The plateau of Tibet is the highest on earth, popularly known as "the roof of the world". On its eastern side are the sources of the Mekong river, which flows into southeast Asia, and China's two major waterways the Yangtze (Chang) and Huang (Yellow River).

The Tibet region is home to several species of wildlife unique to the region, including the yak, and the takin (a relative of the musk ox). The forests of southern Tibet and Sichuan are the home of the red panda. Their relatives, the rare giant panda, live in the bamboo forests of Sichuan, and are closely protected by the government.

Land area 9,526,900 sq km (3,676,300 sq mi)

Major physical features highest point: Mount Everest 8,848 m (29,028 ft); lowest point: Turfan depression –154 m (–505 ft); longest river: Yangtze 5,900 km (3,722 mi)

Population (1994) 1,190,431,106

Form of government Communist state

Largest cities Shanghai (12,320,000); Beijing (capital – 9,750,000); Tianjin (7,790,000); Chongqing (6,511,000); Guangzhou (5,669,000); Shenyang (5,055,000); Wuhan (4,273,000)

Official language Mandarin Chinese

Ethnic composition Han (Chinese) 92.0%; Chuang 1.4%; Manchu 0.9%; Hui 0.8%; Miao 0.7%; Uighur 0.6%; Yi 0.6%; Tuchia 0.5%; Mongolian 0.4%; Tibetan 0.4%; others 1.7%

Religious affiliations nonreligious 71.2%; Chinese folk religion 20.1%; Buddhist 6.0%; Muslim 2.4%; Christian 0.2%; others 0.1%

Currency 1 yuan (Y) = 10 jiao = 100 fen

Economy Gross national product (per capita 1993) US $490; Gross domestic product (1993) US $425,611 million

Life expectancy at birth male 69.0 yr; female 71.0 yr

Major resources Coal, iron ore, petroleum, hydroelectric power, mercury, tin, tungsten, antimony, manganese, aluminum, lead, zinc

Major international organizations ESCAP, IMF, NAM, UN, UNESCO, WHO

China boasts one of the oldest and most advanced civilizations in the world. During the centuries BC the Chinese perfected the wheel, developed a system of writing that still survives today, invented the calendar, developed working in bronze, iron and steel, were the first to use metal coinage and paper money, invented gunpowder and were the first to weave silk into fabric. During the Zhou dynasty, China's most influential teacher and thinker, Confucius (551-479 BC), set the pattern of Chinese philosophy for centuries to come. In 211 BC the Qin ruler Zhao Zheng united the different areas that made up China into one nation and claimed for himself the title *Shi Huangdi* (First Sovereign Emperor). His next ambition was to protect his kingdom with a massive system of interlinked fortifications — the Great Wall of China. When Zhao Zheng died he was buried with 6,000 terracotta figures, the famous "terracotta army" that is one of China's foremost tourist attractions today.

The dynastic system died out in China in the early 20th century with Emperor Puyi, the last of the Manchu dynasty that had ruled China for 268 years. Nineteenth-century government had been corrupt provoking a series of uprisings that escalated into a bitter civil war, punctuated by Japanese domination. National unity was restored by the foundation of the People's Republic of China in 1949 under the Communist leader Mao Zedong, the spirit behind the "Great Leap Forward" and the "Cultural Revolution".

Since 1949, China has been a single-party state, in which the Communist party controls most aspects of daily life through mass-membership organizations such as trade unions, youth leagues, and professional associations. Since the 1970s the economy has moved steadily away from the Soviet-style command economy, toward a market economy where privately owned produce can be sold for a private profit. However, most medium and large-scale industries are still state-owned and run as co-operatives.

Administrative Divisions

(with population for 1990)

MUNICIPALITIES

Beijing	(10,870,000)
Shanghai	(13,510,000)
Tianjin	(8,830,000)

PROVINCES

Anhui	(52,290,000)
Fujian	(30,610,000)
Gansu	(22,930,000)
Guangdong	(63,210,000)
Guizhou	(32,730,000)
Hainan	(6,420,000)
Hebei	(60,280,000)
Heilongjiang	(34,770,000)
Henan	(86,140,000)
Hubei	(54,760,000)
Hunan	(60,600,000)
Jiangsu	(68,170,000)
Jiangxi	(38,280,000)
Jilin	(25,150,000)
Liaoning	(39,980,000)
Qinghai	(4,430,000)
Shaanxi	(32,470,000)
Shandong	(83,430,000)
Shanxi	(28,180,000)
Sichuan	(106,370,000)
Yunnan	(36,750,000)

AUTONOMOUS REGIONS

Inner Mongolia	(21,110,000)
Guangxi	(42,530,000)
Tibet	(2,220,000)
Ningxia	(4,660,000)
Xinjiang	(15,370,000)

municipality
province
autonomous region

HEILONGJIANG

JILIN

LIAONING

INNER
MONGOLIA

BEIJING

Beijing
(Peking)

TIANJIN

HEBEI

SHANXI

SHANDONG

NINGXIA

QINGHAI

GANSU

SHAANXI

HENAN

JIANGSU

SHANGHAI

CHINA

ANHUI

HUBEI

ZHEJIANG

SICHUAN

HUNAN

JIANGXI

FUJIAN

GUIZHOU

YUNNAN

GUANGXI

GUANGDONG

HAINAN

COLOMBIA

Land area 1,141,748 sq km (440,831 sq mi)
Major physical features highest point: Pico Cristóbal Colón 5,800 m (19,029 ft)
Population (1994) 35,577,556
Form of government multiparty republic with two legislative houses
Largest cities Bogotá (capital – 4,923,000); Medellín (1,581,000); Cali (1,624,000); Barranquilla (1,019,000)
Official language Spanish
Ethnic composition mestizo 58.0%; white 20.0%; mulatto 14.0%; black 4.0%; mixed black/Amerindian 3.0%; Amerindian 1.0%

Religious affiliations Roman Catholic 95.0%; others 5.0%
Currency 1 Columbian peso = 100 centavos
Economy Gross national product (per capita 1993) US $1,400; Gross domestic product (1993) US $54,076 million
Life expectancy at birth male 69.3 yr; female 74.9 yr
Major resources petroleum, natural gas, coal, iron ore, coffee, gold, copper, emeralds
Major international organizations ECLAC, GATT, IBRD, IMF, LAIA, NAM, UN, UNESCO, UNHCR, UNPROFOR, WHO

Columbia, named after the explorer Christopher Columbus, has a history of continual unrest extending to the present day. Its prosperity is due to abundant natural resources, traditionally coffee and emeralds, more recently petroleum and illegal trading in drugs.

COMOROS

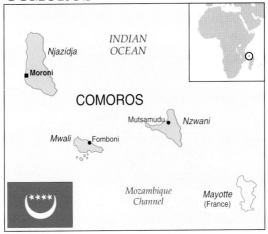

Land area 1,862 sq km (719 sq mi)
Major physical features highest point:
Mount Kartala (Njazidja) 2,361 m (7,746 ft);
largest island: Njazidja 1,148 sq km (443 sq mi)
Population (1994) 530,136
Form of government federal multiparty
republic with one legislative house
Capital city Moroni (22,000)
Official languages Arabic, French
Ethnic composition Comorian
(Bantu/Arab/Malagasy) 96.9%; Makua 1.6%;
French 0.4%; others 1.1%

Official religion Islam
Religious affiliations Sunni Muslim 99.7%;
Christian 0.2%; Baha'i 0.1%
Currency 1 Comorian franc = 100 centimes
Economy Gross national product (per capita
1991) US $500
Life expectancy at birth male 55.6 yr;
female 60.1 yr
Major resources negligible
Major international organizations IBRD,
IMF, NAM, UN, UNESCO, WHO

Comoros is a group of volcanic islands in the Indian Ocean between northern
Madagascar and the African coast. Three out of four islands form an independent republic, but Mayotte remains a French dependency. The islands have almost no mineral
resources and depend on subsistence agriculture. Food crops include cassava, sweet
potatoes and mountain rice, with cloves and vanilla grown as cash crops. Goats and cattle are farmed, and tourism provides important revenue. France is the chief trading
partner and source of aid. In the late 1970s, during a period of political unrest, French
aid was temporarily rejected, and the Comorian economy suffered a catastrophic slump.

CONGO

Land area 342,000 sq km (132,047 sq mi)

Major physical features highest point: Monts de la Lékéti 1,040 m (3,410 ft); longest river: Zaire (part) 4,630 km (2,880 mi)

Population (1994) 2,446,902

Form of government one-party republic with one legislative house

Largest cities Brazzaville (capital – 938,000); Pointe Noire (576,000)

Official language French

Ethnic composition Kongo 51.5%; Teke 17.3%; Mboshi 11.5%; Mbete 4.8%; Punu 3.0%; Sanga 2.7%; Maka 1.8%; Pygmy 1.5%; others 5.9%

Religious affiliations Christian 50.0%; Animist 48.0%; Muslim 2.0%

Currency 1 CFA franc = 100 centimes

Economy Gross national product (per capita 1993) US $950; Gross domestic product (1993) US $2,385 million

Life expectancy at birth male 45.8 yr; female 49.4 yr

Major resources petroleum, timber, potash, lead, zinc, uranium, copper, phosphates, sugar cane, coffee, natural gas

Major international organizations GATT, IBRD, IMF, NAM, UN, UNESCO, WHO

Congo occupies a strip of land running from the western Atlantic coast of Africa into the heart of the continent. It was colonized by the French in the 19th century, who renamed it French Congo, and harshly exploited the area's rich mineral resources. Following independence in 1960, Congo suffered several decades of unrest and dramatic changes of leadership. Political reforms in 1990 laid the foundations for multiparty democratic elections. Present-day Congo encompasses the Angolan enclave of Cabinda.

COSTA RICA

Land area 51,100 sq km (19,730 sq mi)
Major physical feature highest point:
Chirripó 3,820 m (12,533 ft)
Population (1994) 3,342,154
Form of government multiparty republic
with one legislative house
Capital city San José (245,000)
Official language Spanish
Ethnic composition European 87.0%;
mestizo 7.0%; black/mulatto 3.0%; Eastern
Asian 2.0%; Amerindian 1.0%
Official religion Roman Catholicism

Religious affiliations Roman Catholic
95.0%; others 5.0%
Currency 1 Costa Rican colón = 100 céntimos
Economy Gross national product (per capita
1993) US $2,150; Gross domestic product
(1993) US $7,577 million
Life expectancy at birth male 75.8 yr;
female 79.8 yr
Major resources coffee, bananas, timber,
hydroelectric power
Major international organizations BCIE,
CACM, GATT, IMF, UN, UNESCO, WHO

Costa Rica lies on the Central American isthmus between Nicaragua and Panama. The
Pacific and Caribbean coastal belts are lined with mangrove swamps and white, sandy
beaches, rising to a mountainous interior that is prone to earthquakes and volcanic
eruptions. Costa Rica was a Spanish colony from 1570 until independence in 1838. For
much of this period the economy was dependant on coffee exports, but in the last
decade falling coffee prices, combined with earthquake damage, and influxes of
refugees from neighboring war-torn countries have caused widespread hardship.

CROATIA

Land area 56,538 sq km (21,829 sq mi)
Major physical features highest point: within Dinaric Alps 1,831 m (6,005 ft); longest river: Sava (part) 940 km (584 mi)
Population (1994) 4,697,614
Form of government Parliamentary democracy
Capital city Zagreb (931,000)
Official language Serbo-Croat
Ethnic composition Croat 77.9%; Serb 12.2%; others 9.9%
Religious affiliations Roman Catholic 76.5%; Orthodox 11.1%; Slavic Muslim 1.2%; Protestant 0.4%; others 10.8%
Currency 1 Croatian dinar = 100 paras
Economy one of the richer republics of former Yugoslavia, with a developed industrial sector and varied agricultural produce. Tourism was very important before the outbreak of civil war. GNP and GDP not available
Major resources oil, coal, bauxite, iron ore
Major international organizations AEA, IBRD, IMF, UN, UNESCO, WHO

Before the outbreak of civil war in 1989 Croatia was the second most prosperous region of former Yugoslavia, after Slovenia. Today it is still suffering extensive war damage.

CUBA

Land area 110,861 sq km (42,804 sq mi)
Major physical features highest point:
Turquino 2,005 m (6,578 ft); longest river:
Cauto 249 km (155 mi)
Population (1994) 11,064,344
Form of government one-party republic
with one legislative house
Largest cities Havana (capital – 2,096,000);
Santiago de Cuba (405,000); Camagüey
(283,000); Guantánamo (200,000)
Official language Spanish
Ethnic composition mulatto 51.0%; white
37.0%; black 11.0%; Chinese 1.0%

Religious affiliations nonreligious 55.1%;
Roman Catholic 39.6%; Afro-Cuban 1.6%;
Protestant 3.3%
Currency 1 Cuban peso = 100 centavos
Economy Gross national product (per capita
1991) US $1,000
Life expectancy at birth male 74.7 yr;
female 79.2 yr
Major resources sugar, tobacco, timber,
fisheries, citrus fruits, coffee, nickel
Major international organizations ECLAC,
GATT, LAES, UN, UNESCO, WHO

Cuba is an island state in the Caribbean directly south of Florida. It consists of the main
island of Cuba and a much smaller island to the south called La Isla de la Juventud (Isle
of Youth). Columbus landed in Cuba in 1492 and it became one of the earliest Spanish
colonies in the region. It achieved independence in 1899, and was governed by a series
of corrupt dictators until 1959 when a communist revolutionary movement led by Fidel
Castro seized power. With the support of the Soviet Union, Castro remodeled Cuba as a
personal dictatorship run along Soviet lines, but raising considerably the living standards of the poor. Since the breakup of the Soviet Union, the Cuban economy has lost a
major supplier of essential fuel and foodstuffs, and has slumped badly.

CYPRUS

Land area 9,251 sq km (3,572)
Major physical feature highest point: Mount Olympus 1,951 m (6,403 ft)
Population (1994) 730,084
Form of government multiparty republic with one legislative house [Turkish Republic not recognized internationally]
Largest cities Nicosia (capital – 169,000); Limassol (132,000); Famagusta (39,000)
Official languages Greek, Turkish
Ethnic composition Greek 78%; Turkish 18%; others (mainly British) 4%
Religious affiliations Christian (mostly Greek Orthodox) 78%; Muslim 18%; others 4%
Currency 1 Cyprus pound (C£) = 100 cents [1 Turkish lira (LT) = 100 kurus]
Economy Gross national product (per capita 1991) US $8,640
Life expectancy at birth male 74.0 yr; female 78.6 yr
Major resources tourism, citrus fruit, olives, vegetables, copper, asbestos, timber, salt
Major international organizations EBRD, GATT, IMF, UN, UNESCO, WHO

Note: Where possible, data is given for the whole of Cyprus; Turkish-sector information is in square brackets

Cyprus is the third largest island in the Mediterranean, lying south of Turkey and west of Syria. Politically the island is divided by a long-running conflict between Cypriots of Greek descent, who make up the majority, and a minority of Turkish Cypriots. The Turkish sector, about one fifth of the population, is mainly dependent on agriculture, but in recent decades the Greek sector has enjoyed impressive growth in tourism and industry. Prosperity and economic growth was severely set back by the Turkish invasion of Cyprus in 1974. Since then, many Cypriots from both communities have left their communities to work abroad, particularly in Britain and the Middle East.

CZECH REPUBLIC

Land area   78,865 sq km (30,450 sq mi)
Major physical features   highest point: Mt Snezka (Sudetic Mountains) 1,603 m (5,259 ft); longest rivers: Elbe/Labe (part) 1,165 km (724 m), Vltava 430 km (267 mi)
Population   (1994) 10,408,280
Form of government   parliamentary democracy
Largest cities   Prague (capital – 1,216,000); Brno (392,000); Ostrava (332,000); Plzen (175,000)
Official language   Czech
Ethnic composition   Czech 94.4%; Slovak 3%; others 2.6%

Religious affiliations   atheist 39.8%; Roman Catholic 39.2%; Protestant 4.6%; orthodox 3.0%; others 13.4%
Currency   1 koruna (Kĕs) = 100 halura
Economy   Gross national product (per capita 1993) US $2,710; Gross domestic product (1993) US $31,613 million
Life expectancy at birth   male 69.4 yr; female 77.0 yr
Major resources   coal, lignite, hops (beer), kaolin, clay, graphite, iron ore, tourism, glass
Major international organizations   GATT, IBRD, IMF, UNESCO, UNPROFOR, WHO

The Czech Republic came into being in 1993 when the former state of Czechoslovakia split into two new states (the other being Slovakia). Most of the newly formed Czech Republic occupied the territory of the former kingdoms of Bohemia, Moravia, and Silesia.

DENMARK

Land area 43,093 sq km (16,638 sq mi)
Major physical features highest point: Yding Skovhøj (central Jutland) 173 m (568 ft); largest island: Sjælland 7,104 sq km (2,708 sq mi)
Population (1994) 5,187,821
Form of government multiparty constitutional monarchy with one legislative house
Largest cities Copenhagen (capital — 1,337,000); Århus (271,000); Odense (181,000); Ålborg (157,000)
Official language Danish
Ethnic composition Danish 97.2%; Turkish 0.5%; other Scandinavians 0.4%; others 1.9%
Religious affiliations Lutheran 90.6%; Roman Catholic 0.5%; Jewish 0.1%; others 8.8%
Currency 1 Danish krone (DKr) = 100 Øre
Economy Gross national product (per capita 1993) US $26,730; Gross domestic product (1993) US $117,587 million
Life expectancy at birth male 72.9 yr; female 78.6 yr
Major resources meat and dairy produce, fisheries
Major international organizations CBSS, EU, GATT, IMF, NATO, UN, UNPROFOR, WHO

Denmark is the smallest of the Scandinavian countries in northern Europe; it also enjoys the highest standard of living in the European Community. Its prosperity is based on high-tech agriculture, and a distribution system that exports Danish meat, fish and dairy produce all over Europe. Modern small-scale industry is also very profitable. Danes pay very high income tax funding extensive welfare and educational programs.

DJIBOUTI

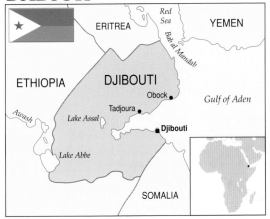

Land area 23,200 sq km (8,950 sq mi)
Major physical features highest point: Musa Ali Terara 2,063 m (6,768 ft); lowest point: Lake Assal –150m (–492 ft)
Population (1993) 695,000
Form of government one-party republic with one legislative house
Capital city Djibouti (290,000)
Official languages Arabic, French
Ethnic composition Somali 60.0%; Afar 35.0%; French, Arab, Ethiopian & Italian 5.0%

Religious affiliations Sunni Muslim 94%; Roman Catholic 4%; Protestant 1%; Orthodox 1%
Currency 1 Djibouti franc = 100 centimes
Economy Gross national product (per capita 1991) US $1,000
Life expectancy at birth male 47.4 yr; female 51.1 yr
Major resources geothermal power, fisheries, port facilities
Major industrial organizations IBRD, IDB, IMF, NAM, UN, UNESCO, WHO

Djibouti is the smallest country in northern Africa, a desert republic on the east coast strategically sited to control sea access between the Indian Ocean and the Red Sea (leading to the Suez Canal). Natural resources are limited and the arid climate is not able to support enough pasture and livestock to meet the domestic demand for food. The economy depends on trade and services (particularly trans-shipment of imports and exports to Ethiopia, Somalia, and other countries in the region). Foreign aid is supplied by Djibouti's major trading partners — notably France (the former colonial power), Italy and Saudi Arabia. However, conditions are very poor, drought and famine never far away, and almost half of recorded deaths of children under 10 years old are caused by malnutrition, dehydration or accidental poisoning.

DOMINICA

Land area 750 sq km (290 sq mi)
Major physical feature highest point: Morne Diablotin 1,447 m (4,747 ft)
Population (1994) 87,696
Form of government multiparty republic with one legislative house
Capital city Roseau (21,000)
Official language English
Ethnic composition black 91.2%; mixed 6.6%; Amerindian 1.5%; white 0.5%; others 0.2%
Religious affiliations Roman Catholic 76.9%; Protestant 15.5%; others 7.6%
Currency 1 East Caribbean dollar (EC$) = 100 cents
Economy Gross national product (per capita 1991) US $2,440
Life expectancy at birth male 74.1 yr; female 79.9 yr
Major resources bananas, citrus fruit, coconuts, bay leaves, vegetables, vanilla
Major international organizations CARICOM, ELAC, GATT, IBRD, IMF, NAM, UN, UNESCO, WHO

Dominica is an island republic in the Leeward Island chain lying in the eastern Caribbean between Guadeloupe and Martinique. The island was originally volcanic, though no longer active, but vents and hot springs in the high central mountain ranges are reminders of its origins. During the 18th century the British and French fought over possession of the island, with the British finally taking possession in 1783. Dominica became self-governing in 1967, and gained full independence in 1978. Today tropical fruit and other food crops are the mainstay of the economy, and tourism may become increasingly important. At present tourist potential is hampered by the rugged coastline (unlike the sandy beaches on other islands) and lack of an international airport.

DOMINICAN REPUBLIC

Land area 48,443 sq km (18,704 sq mi)

Major physical feature highest point: Pico Duarte 3,175 m (10,417 ft)

Population (1994) 7,600,000

Form of government multiparty republic with two legislative houses

Largest cities Santo Domingo (capital – 1,601,000); Santiago (308,000); La Romana (91,600)

Official language Spanish

Ethnic composition mulatto 73.0%; white 16.0%; black 11.0%

Religious affiliations Roman Catholic 91.9%

Currency 1 Dominican Republic peso (RD$) = 100 centavos

Economy Gross national product (per capita 1993) US $1,230; Gross domestic product (1993) US $9,510 million

Life expectancy at birth male 66.2 yr; female 70.6 yr

Major resources sugar cane, tobacco, salt, coffee, bauxite, nickel, tourism

Major international organizations CARICOM, ECLAC, IMF, UN, UNESCO, WHO

Dominican Republic occupies the eastern part of the Caribbean island of Hispaniola — the western part is occupied by its much smaller neighbor Haiti. Hispaniola is a mountainous tropical island with a varied landscape ranging from lush vegetation in the north to arid scrubland in the south. The economy depends on agriculture, with cash crops of sugar, tobacco and coffee grown on plantations for the export market. Small deposits of minerals support mining and processing industries, and tourism is being developed.

ECUADOR

Land area 269,178 sq km (103,930 sq mi)
Major physical features highest point:
Chimborazo 6,310 m (20,702 ft); longest river:
Napo (part) 1,100 km (700 mi)
Population (1994) 10,677,067
Form of government multiparty republic
with one legislative house
Largest cities Guayaquil (1,508,000); Quito
(capital – 1,101,000); Cuenca (195,000);
Ambato (124,000)
Official language Spanish
Ethnic composition mestizo 55%; Indian
25%; Spanish 10%; black 10%

Religious affiliations Roman Catholic
95.0%; others 5.0%
Currency 1 Sucre (S/.) = 100 centavos
Economy Gross national product (per capita
1993) US $1,200; Gross domestic product
(1993) US $14,421 million
Life expectancy at birth male 67.5 yr;
female 72.6 yr
Major resources petroleum, bananas,
cocoa, coffee, shrimp
Major international organizations ECLAC,
IBRD, IMF, LAIA, NAM, UN, UNESCO, WHO

Ecuador lies on the west coast of South America between Colombia and Peru; as its
name suggests, the equator runs through it. The territory also includes the Galapagos
islands, which lie about 1,000 km (600 mi) out in the Pacific. Mainland Ecuador is
mountainous and prone to earthquakes — two parallel chains of the Andes run from
north to south, and there are volcanic hills in the coastal areas. There are rich
resources of oil, but growth of the petroleum industry is hampered by natural disasters.

EGYPT

Land area 997,739 sq km (385,229 sq mi)
Major physical features highest point:
Mount Catherine 2,637 m (8,652 ft); longest
river: Nile (part) 6,690 km (4,160 mi)
Population (1994) 60,765,028
Form of government Single-party republic
with one legislative house
Largest cities Cairo (capital – 6,663,000);
Alexandria (3,295,000); Giza (2,096,000)
Official language Arabic
Ethnic composition Egyptian 99.8%; others
0.2%
Official religion Islam

Religious affiliations Sunni Muslim 94.0%;
Christian 6.0%
Currency 1 Egyptian pound (LE) = 100 pias-
tres = 1,000 millièmes
Economy Gross national product (per capita
1993) US $660; Gross domestic product (1993)
US $35,784 million
Life expectancy at birth male 58.9 yr;
female 62.8 yr
Major resources petroleum, natural gas,
iron ore, phosphates, manganese, limestone
Major international organizations GATT,
IMF, OAPEC, UN, UNESCO, UNPROFOR, WHO

Egypt, in the northeastern corner of Africa, is a desert land with one enormous lush valley running the entire length of the country on either side of the river Nile. This valley
boasts one of the oldest continuous civilizations in the world. Today Egypt's economy
depends on oil, revenues from the Suez canal and tourism. Foreign debt is enormous.

EL SALVADOR

Land area 21,041 sq km (8,124 sq mi)
Major physical features highest point:
Izalco 2,386 m (7,828 ft); longest river: Lempa
320 km (200 mi)
Population (1994) 5,752,511
Form of government multiparty republic
with one legislative house
Largest cities San Salvador (capital –
1,522,000); Santa Ana (239,000); San Miguel
(192,000)
Official language Spanish
Ethnic composition mestizo 94.0%;
Amerindian 5.0%; white 1.0%

Religious affiliations Roman Catholic
75.0%; others 25.0%
Currency 1 colón = 100 centavos
Economy Gross national product (per capita
1993) US $1,320; Gross domestic product
(1993) US $7,625 million
Life expectancy at birth male 64.4 yr;
female 69.7 yr
Major resources coffee, cotton, corn (maize)
sugar cane, hydroelectric power
Major international organizations BCIE,
ECLAC, GATT, IAEA, IBRD, IMF, UN,
UNESCO, WHO

El Salvador is the smallest and most densely populated country in Central America. The terrain is mountainous and volcanic, with fertile grasslands and deciduous forests on the coastal plains. The economy is based on agriculture, and coffee is a vital cash crop. Between 1979 and 1992 the left-wing Martí Front for National Liberation (FLMN) fought a bloody civil war against successive governments, leading to the deaths of tens of thousands of people. The conflict ended when the United Nations sponsored a successful peace conference in Mexico, and the last FLMN troops were disbanded in December 1992. For many years civil war has prevented foreign investment in industry.

EQUATORIAL GUINEA

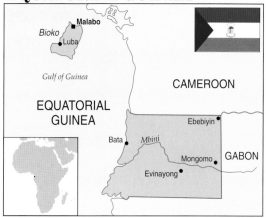

Land area   28,051 sq km (10,830 sq mi)

Major physical features   highest point: Pico de Santa Isabel 3,007 m (9,685 ft); largest island: Bioko 2,017 sq km (779 sq mi)

Population   (1994) 409,550

Form of government   multiparty republic with one legislative house

Capital city   Malabo (37,000)

Official language   Spanish

Ethnic composition   Fang 72.0%; Bubi 14.7%; Duala 2.7%; Ibibio 1.3%; Maka 1.3%; others 8.0%

Religious affiliations   Roman Catholic 88.8%; traditional beliefs 4.6%; Muslim 0.5%; others 0.2%; none 5.9%

Currency   1 CFA franc = 100 centimes

Economy   Gross national product (per capita 1991) US $330

Life expectancy at birth   male 50.0 yr; female 54.3 yr

Major resources   cocoa, timber, coffee, fisheries, petroleum, natural gas

Major international organizations   IBRD, IMF, NAM, UN, UNESCO, WHO

The mainland of Equatorial Guinea faces the Gulf of Guinea on the western shore of Africa. The territory also includes five islands in the Gulf, the largest of which are Bioko (volcanic) and Annobón. Formerly a Spanish colony, Equatorial Guinea gained its independence in 1968, and held its first democratic elections in 1982. Agriculture is vital to the economy, and growth of cash crops for export leaves little space to grow staple foods. Malnutrition is common, manufacturing underdeveloped, and the transportation and communication network very poor. Spanish subsidies are needed to keep the balance of trade positive. Very recently deposits of oil and natural gas have been discovered, and their exploitation may alter the fortunes of the country.

ERITREA

Land area   121,320 sq km (46,842 sq mi)
Climate   hot, dry desert strip
Major physical feature   highest point:
Monte Soira 2,989 m (9,806.9 ft)
Population   (1994) 3,782,543
Form of government   transitional
Capital city   Asmara (358,000)
Official languages   Tigrinya and Arabic

Religious affiliations   Muslim; Coptic
Christian; Roman Catholic; Protestant (figures not available)
Currency   1 birr (Br) = 100 cents
Life expectancy at birth   male 44.0 yr;
female 48.0 yr
Major resources   offshore oil (unexploited)
Major international organizations   UN

Eritrea was recognized by the United Nations as an independent state on April 27, 1993, after a 30-year war with Ethiopia that left the new nation impoverished, famine-stricken and without an infrastructure. It is currently controlled by a transitional government that aims to hold democratic elections before mid-1997. A former Italian colony, and under British rule 1942–52, Eritrea became part of Ethiopia when the European empires dissolved during the 1960s. The struggle for independence reached a climax in 1991 when other discontented groups in Ethiopia joined with the Eritrean People's Liberation Front to bring down the Mengistu government that had seized power from the aging Ethiopian emperor in 1974. Eritrea occupies a powerful strategic position, controlling all points of access to the Red Sea and beyond. Secession from Ethiopia leaves the larger country landlocked, and dependent on Eritrea for access to foreign trade. In the long term Eritrea has plans to develop tourism along the Red Sea as well as an offshore oil industry, and offshore fishing.

ESTONIA

Land area 45,100 sq km (17,400 sq mi)
Major physical features highest point: Munamägi 318 m (1,042 ft); largest lake: Lake Peipus (part) 3,548 sq km (1,370 sq mi)
Population (1994) 1,616,882
Form of government multiparty republic with one legislative house
Largest cities Tallinn (capital – 499,000); Tartu (114,000); Narva (82,000); Kohtla-Järve (77,000)
Official language Estonian
Ethnic composition Estonian 61.5%; Russian 30.3%; Ukrainian 3.2%; Belorussian 1.8%; Finnish 1.1%; others 2.1%
Religious affiliations mainly Lutheran, with Eastern Orthodox and Baptist minorities
Currency 1 Estonian kroon = 100 cents
Economy Gross national product (per capita 1993) US $3,080; Gross domestic product (1993) US $5,092 million
Life expectancy at birth male 65.0 yr; female 75.1 yr
Major resources beef and dairy cattle, timber, bituminous shale, peat, amber
Major international organizations CBSS, IBRD, IMF, UN, UNESCO, WHO

Estonia is the northernmost of the three Baltic republics, formerly part of the Soviet Union. The Estonian people speak a language similar to Finnish, and share a cultural heritage with the Finns that survived years of foreign domination. Following independence in 1991, the Estonian government introduced a program of market reforms that is transforming the economy — inflation is low, the private sector is growing rapidly, and foreign trade has shifted rapidly from Russia and Eastern Europe to the West.

ETHIOPIA

Land area 1,119,683 sq km (433,789 sq mi)
Major physical feature highest point: Ras Dashan 4,620 m (15,158 ft)
Population (1994) 54,927,108
Form of government one-party republic with one legislative house
Largest cities Addis Ababa (capital – 1,913,000); Dire Dawa (127,000)
Official language Amharic
Ethnic composition Oromo 40.0%; Amhara and Tigrean 32.0%; Sidamo 9.0%; Shankella 6.0%; Somah 6.0%; Afar 4.0%; Gurage 2.0%; others 1.0%

Religious affiliations Muslim 45–50%; Ethiopian Orthodox 35–40%; Animist 12.0%; others 5.0%
Currency 1 Ethiopian birr (Br) = 100 cents
Economy Gross national product (per capita 1993) US $100; Gross domestic product (1993) US $5,750 million
Life expectancy at birth male 51.0 yr; female 54.4 yr
Major resources coffee, small reserves of gold, platinum, copper, potash
Major international organizations IBRD, IMF, NAM, UN, UNESCO, UNHCR, WHO

Ethiopia is a massive plateau in northeast Africa, cut in half from north to south by the East African Rift Valley. It is one of the poorest and least developed countries in Africa, scarred and torn by drought, famine and civil war with Eritrea, which gained independence in April 1993. Since then Ethiopia has been landlocked, a situation that can only exacerbate its existing economic problems. Subsistence agriculture provides 80% of employment, and coffee is the only significant export.

FED. STATES OF MICRONESIA

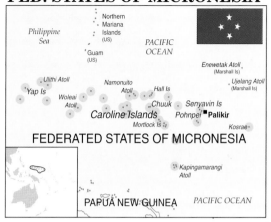

Land area 702 sq km (271.04 sq mi)
Population (1994) 120,347
Form of government federal republic
Capital city Palikir (on the island of Pohnpei)
Official language English
Ethnic composition nine ethnic Micronesian and polynesian groups
Religious affiliations Christian (Roman Catholic, Protestant, Assembly of God, Jehovah's Witness, Seventh-day Adventist, Latter-Day Saints), Baha'i
Currency 1 US dollar = 100 cents
Economy Gross national product (per capita 1994) US $980
Life expectancy at birth male 65.7 yr; female 69.6yr
Major resources fisheries, sea-bed minerals, copra, black pepper, timber
Major international organizations IBRD, IMF, UN, WHO

The Federated States of Micronesia are a group of scattered volcanic islands in the western Pacific Ocean, including the eastern and central Caroline Islands. They have a hot rainy climate encouraging lush tropical vegetation and extensive rainforest. In 1989 all the islands were released from a United States-administered UN trusteeship, and became a federal republic in free association with the United States; in 1992 they became an independent republic. The main economic activities among the indigenous peoples are subsistence farming and fishing. In the past, the islands depended greatly on United States' aid, grants and military spending. In the future, however, they intend to become more self-sufficient, developing tourism and generating more income from the sale of fishing rights and cash crops.

FIJI

Land area 18,274 sq km (7,056 sq mi)
Major physical features largest island: Viti Levu 10,429 sq km (4,027 sq mi); highest point: Mount Tomanivi (on Viti Levu) 1,323 m (4,341 ft)
Population (1994) 764,382
Form of government multiparty republic with two legislative houses
Capital city Suva (141,000)
Official language English
Ethnic composition Fijian 48.9%; Asian Indian 46.2%; others 4.9%

Religious affiliations Christian 52.9%; Hindu 38.1%; Muslim 7.8%; Sikh 0.7%; others 0.5%
Currency 1 Fiji dollar (F$) = 100 cents
Economy Gross national product (per capita 1991) US $1,830
Life expectancy at birth male 62.9 yr; female 67.5 yr
Major resources sugar, tourism, timber, fisheries, gold, copper
Major international organizations GATT, IMF, UN, UNESCO, WHO

Fiji is an isolated archipelago in the southwestern Pacific some 2,100 km (1,300 mi) north of Auckland, New Zealand. Most of the islands are volcanic with the two largest, Viti Levu and Vanua Levu, accounting for almost nine tenths of the land area, and the vast majority of the population. Fiji was a British colony from 1879 until it achieved independence in 1970. Agriculture, tourism and light industry support the economy.

FINLAND

Land area 338,145 sq km (130,559 sq mi)
Major physical features highest point: Haltiatunturi (northern Finland) 1,328 m (4,357 ft); longest river: Kemi 483 km (300 mi)
Population (1994) 5,068,931
Form of government multiparty republic with one legislative house
Largest cities Helsinki (capital – 498,000); Turku (160,000); Tampere (174,000)
Official languages Finnish, Swedish
Ethnic composition Finnish 93.6%; Swedish 6.0%; others 0.4%
Religious affiliations Lutheran 88.7%; Finnish (Greek) Orthodox 1.1%; unaffiliated 9.3%; others 0.9%
Currency 1 markka (Fmk) = 100 pennia
Economy Gross national product (per capita 1993) US $19,300; Gross domestic product (1993) US $74,124 million
Life expectancy at birth male 72.2yr; female 79.9 yr
Major resources timber, copper, zinc, nickel, silver, fisheries, peat
Major international organizations CBSS, EU, GATT, IMF, OECD, UN, UNESCO, UNHCR, UNPROFOR, WHO

Finland is the most northerly country in Europe, with one third of its land area lying within the Arctic Circle. It is a prosperous, modern, industrialized free-market economy, using its great forests as the mainstay of a huge lumber and pulp export business.

FRANCE

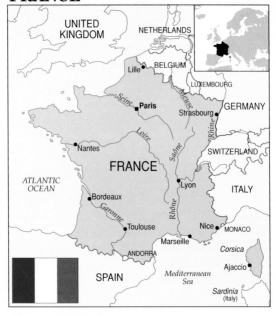

Land area   543,965 sq km (210,026 sq mi)

Major physical features   highest point: Mont Blanc 4,807 m (15,770 ft); longest river: Loire 1,020 km (630 mi)

Population   (1994) 57,840,445

Form of government   multiparty republic with two legislative houses

Largest cities   Paris (capital – 9,319,000); Lyon (1,262,000); Marseille (1,087,000)

Official language   French

Ethnic composition   French 90.6% (including Occitan 2.7%, Alsatian 2.3%, Breton 1.0%, Catalan 0.4%); Algerian 1.5%; Portuguese 1.4%; Moroccan 0.8%; Spanish 0.6%; Italian 0.6%; others 4.5%

Religious affiliations   Roman Catholic 76.4%; other Christians 3.7%; Muslim 3.0%; nonreligious and others 16.9%

Currency   1 franc (F) = 100 centimes

Economy   Gross national product (per capita 1993) US $22,490; Gross domestic product (1993) US $1,251,689 million

Life expectancy at birth   male 74.3 yr; female 82.3 yr

Major resources   agricultural produce (cereals, dairy products, wine, fruit), timber, fisheries, bauxite, potash, rock salt, uranium

Major international organizations   EU, GATT, G-7, IBRD, IMF, NATO, UN, UNESCO, UNHCR, UNPROFOR, WHO

France is the largest country in western Europe and has a long history of cultural influence, both within Europe and across the world, as a result of its former colonial power. More recently, its role as a founding member of the European Community has helped to shape much of European economic policy.

France became a republic in 1789 after toppling the unpopular Bourbon monarchy. In 1804 the young Corsican general Napoleon Bonaparte seized power, expanding the French Empire enormously and establishing the prefecture system of local government, the Bank of France, and the Napoleonic Code, the basis of modern French law. In the period before World War I France continued to expand its territory overseas, but the war brought heavy losses, and the Nazi invasion of 1940 during World War II was another crushing blow to a nation that had scarcely recovered from the previous conflict.

Post-war France was dominated by the figure of General de Gaulle who set about rebuilding French industry (almost totally destroyed in the war) and revived prosperity with the newly established European Community, a common market of European trade. Since the 1950s the French economy has enjoyed a high rate of growth, and has risen to be the world's fourth greatest industrial power (after the US, Japan and Germany). Its prosperity rests on steel, automobiles and aircraft, textiles, food processing, perfume, fashion and financial services. It also has an excellent tradition of public education and a vigorous publishing industry.

French Overseas Departments and Territories

(with population)

Guadeloupe, colony since 1635, overseas department from 1946, administrative region from 1974.
Population for 1990 as follows:

St. Martin	(28,518)
St. Barthélemy	(5,038)
Basse-Terre	(149,943)
Grande-Terre	(177,570)
Îles des Saintes	(2,036)
La Désirade	(1,610)
Marie-Galante	(13,463)

French Guiana, colony since 1817, overseas department from 1946, administrative region from 1974.
Population for 1990 (114,808)

Martinique, colony since 1635, overseas department from 1946, and administrative region from 1974.
Population for 1990 (359,579)

Réunion, colony from 1638, overseas department from 1946, and administrative region from 1974.
Population for 1990 (597,828)

Regions of France

Overseas Departments and Territories (cont)

(with population)

Mayotte, colony 1843-1914, when it became an overseas territory, Territorial collectivity from 1976. Population for 1991 (94,410)

St. Pierre and Miquelon, colony 1816-1976, overseas department 1976-85, now a Territorial Collectivity. Population for 1990 (6,392)

Southern and Antarctic Territories, created in 1955 to comprise the Kerguelen and Crozet archipelagoes, the islands of St. Paul and Amsterdam and Terre Adélie.

New Caledonia, annexed by France in 1853, became an overseas territory in 1958. Population for 1989 (164,173)

French Polynesia, French protectorate from 1843, and overseas territory since 1958. Population for 1988 (188,814)

Wallis and Futuna, French dependencies from 1842, and overseas territories since 1961. Population for 1990 (13,705) Wallis (8,973); Futuna (4,732)

Regions of France

(with population for 1990)

Region	Population	Region	Population
Alsace	(1,624,400)	Île-de-France	(10,660,600)
Aquitaine	(2,795,800)	Languedoc-Roussillon	(2,115,000)
Auvergne	(1,321,200)	Limousin	(722,900)
Basse-Normandie	(1,391,300)	Lorraine	(2,305,700)
Bourgogne	(1,609,700)	Midi-Pyrénées	(2,430,700)
Bretagne	(2,795,600)	Nord-Pas-de-Calais	(3,965,100)
Centre	(2,371,000)	Pays de la Loire	(3,059,100)
Champagne-Ardenne	(1,347,800)	Picardie	(1,810,700)
Corse	(250,400)	Poitou-Charentes	(1,595,100)
Franche-Comté	(1,097,300)	Provence-Alpes-Côte d'Azur	(4,257,900)
Haute-Normandie	(1,737,200)	Rhône-Alpes	(5,350,700)

GABON

Land area 267,667 sq km (103,347 sq mi)

Major physical feature highest point: Mont Iboundji 1,575 m (5,176 ft)

Population (1994) 1,139,006

Form of government multiparty republic with one legislative house

Capital city Libreville (830,000)

Official language French

Ethnic composition Fang 35.5%; Mpongwe 15.1%; Mbete 14.2%; Punu 11.5%; others 23.7%

Religious affiliations Roman Catholic 65.2%; Protestant 18.8%; African Christian 12.1%; traditional beliefs 2.9%; Muslim 0.8%; others 0.2%

Currency 1 CFA franc = 100 centimes

Economy Gross national product (per capita 1993) US $4,960; Gross domestic product (1993) US $5,420 million

Life expectancy at birth male 51.9 yr; female 57.5 yr

Major resources petroleum, manganese, uranium, gold, timber, coffee, cocoa, oil palm

Major international organizations GATT, IMF, NAM, OPEC, UN, UNESCO, WHO

Gabon lies on the equator on the west coast of Africa. A former French colony, Gabon gained independence in 1960, and since then has built up a profitable export economy based on mining and processing the country's considerable mineral resources. Manufacturing industries are limited to processing offshore petroleum and timber.

GAMBIA

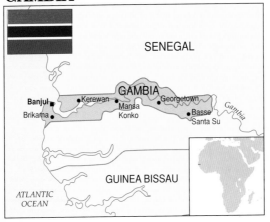

Land area 10,689 sq km (4,127 sq mi)
Major physical feature longest river: Gambia (part) 1,100 km (700 mi)
Population (1993) 1,025,687
Form of government multiparty republic with one legislative house
Capital city Banjul (150,000)
Official language English
Ethnic composition Gambian 99.0% (Mandinka 42.0%, Fula 18.0%, Wolof 16.0%, Jula 10.0%, Serahuli 9.0%, others 4.0%); non-Gambian 1.0%

Religious affiliations Muslim 90.0%; Christian 9.0%; traditional beliefs 1.0%
Currency 1 dalasi (D) = 100 butut
Economy Gross national product (per capita 1993) US $350; Gross domestic product (1993) US $6,084 million
Life expectancy at birth male 47.8 yr; female 52.4 yr
Major resources groundnuts (peanuts), fisheries, palm kernels, tourism
Major international organizations GATT, IMF, NAM, UN, UNESCO, WHO

The Gambia is a tiny state on the west African coast, forming an enclave along the banks and estuary of the Gambia river, and surrounded on three sides by Senegal. The river dominates the country, whose landscape consists of the wide river valley (frequently flooded and some of which is permanently swampland) flanked by low hills, mostly cleared for agriculture, and sandy plateaus. Gambia has few mineral resources and most of the population is employed in subsistence agriculture or fishing. More than half of the country's export revenue is earned by groundnuts, and of palm kernels also make a major contribution. Processing these local crops accounts for the country's very limited manufacturing industries.

GEORGIA

Land area 69,700 sq km (26,900 sq mi)

Major physical features highest point: Shkhara 5,068 m (16,627 ft); longest river: Kura (part) 1,510 km (940 mi)

Population (1994) 5,6814,025

Form of government multiparty republic with one legislative house

Largest cities Tbilisi (capital – 1,279,000); Kutaisi (238,000); Rustavi (162,000); Batumi (138,000); Sukhumi (120,000)

Official language Georgian

Ethnic composition Georgian 70.1%; Armenian 8.1%; Russian 6.3%; Azeri 5.7%; Ossetian 3.0%; Abkhaz 1.8%; others 5.0%

Religious affiliations Georgian Orthodox 65.0%; Russian Orthodox 10.0%; Muslim 11.0%; Armenian Orthodox 8.0%; others 6.0%

Currency coupons were introduced in 1993, to be followed by a new currency called the lari

Economy Gross national product (per capita 1993) US $580; Gross domestic product (1993) US $2,994 million

Life expectancy at birth male 69.2 yr; female 76.7 yr

Major resources timber, citrus fruit, tea, grapes, tourism, manganese, copper

Major international organizations BSEC, IMF, UN, UNESCO, WHO

Georgia is a small mountainous republic at the eastern end of the Black Sea, north of Turkey. Following independence from the Soviet Union in 1991, Georgia refused to join the newly formed CIS, preferring to restructure politically and economically without the help of other former Soviet states. Its economy is based on tourism to the Black Sea coast, traditional exports of citrus fruits, tea, fine wines, and abundant hydropower.

GERMANY

Land area 356,954 sq km (137,820 sq mi)
Major physical features highest point: Zugspitze 2,963 m (9,720 ft); longest rivers: Danube (part) 2,850 km (1,770 mi), Rhine (part) 1,320 km (820 mi), Elbe (part) 1,165 km (724 mi); largest lake: Lake Constance (part) 540 sq km (210 sq mi)
Population (1994) 81,087,506
Form of government federal multiparty republic with two legislative houses
Largest cities Berlin (capital – 3,446,000); Hamburg (1,669,000); Munich (1,229,000); Cologne (957,000); Essen (627,000); Frankfurt (654,000); Dortmund (601,000); Dusseldorf (578,000); Stuttgart (592,000)
Official language German
Ethnic composition German 95.1%; Turkish 2.3%; Italians 0.7%; Greeks 0.4%; Poles 0.4%;

others (including refugees from former Yugoslavia) 1.1%
Religious affiliations Lutheran/Reformed Protestant 45.0%; Roman Catholic 37.0%; unaffiliated and others 18.0%
Currency 1 Deutschmark = 100 Pfennig
Economy Gross national product (per capita 1993) US $23,560; Gross domestic product (1993) US $1,910,760 million
Life expectancy at birth male 73.2 yr; female 79.6 yr
Major resources grapes, dairy produce, hops, meat products, timber, lignite, iron ore, coal, potash, uranium, copper, natural gas, salt, nickel
Major international organizations CBSS, EU, G-7, GATT, IMF, NATO, UN, UNESCO, UNHCR, WHO

93

Germany is Europe's second most populous country and occupies a central position on the continent, sharing borders with nine other nations. For centuries the Germany we know today was a patchwork of rival city-states, principalities and kingdoms that only slowly coalesced into a loose confederation. Unity achieved at the Congress of Vienna 1814-15 was shortlived. At the end of World War II Germany lay in ruins, divided between the Eastern and Western blocs.

From 1945 until 1990 the gulf between the two Germanys widened. West Germany developed into a powerful and prosperous capitalist nation, eventually becoming the wealthiest nation in Europe, third wealthiest in the world (after Japan and the United States). It gained a world-wide reputation as a leading exporter of heavy engineering, automobiles, electronics and chemicals. Low inflation, efficient modern industry, and a strong work ethic were the keys to success in the West. Meanwhile the East remained an agricultural community functioning as a cooperative rather than as a free-market economy, and using out-of-date inefficient equipment.

When the collapse of communism in Eastern Europe made reunification possible, it made a dramatic impact on the culture and economy of each state. East German infrastructure was very poor (communications and transportation were decades behind those in the West) and its industries were heavily polluting the atmosphere and causing significant environmental damage. Replacing old infrastructure with modern new systems in a reunited Germany is stretching state resources to the limit, and the tensions between rich and poor dominate current German politics.

Länder (States) of the Republic

(with populations for 1993)

Baden-Württemberg	(10,149,000)	**North Rhine-Westphalia**	
Bavaria	(11,770,000)		(17,679,000)
Berlin	(3,466,000)	**Rhineland-Palatinate**	(3,881,000)
Brandenburg	(2,543,000)	**Saarland**	(1,084,000)
Bremen	(686,000)	**Saxony**	(4,641,000)
Hamburg	(1,689,000)	**Saxony-Anhalt**	(2,797,000)
Hessen	(5,923,000)	**Schleswig-Holstein**	(2,680,000)
Lower Saxony	(7,578,000)	**Thuringia**	(2,546,000)
Mecklenburg-West Pomerania			
	(1,865,000)		

GHANA

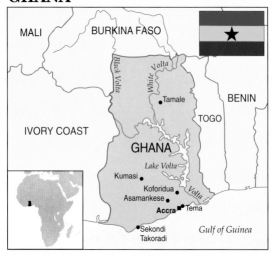

Land area 238,533 sq km (92,098 sq mi)
Major physical features highest point:
Mount Afadjoto 885 m (2,903 ft); largest lake:
Lake Volta 8,462 sq km (3,275 sq mi)
Population (1994) 17,225,185
Form of government republic with a
military government
Largest cities Accra (capital – 965,000);
Kumasi (489,000); Tema (191,000); Tamale
(168,000); Sekondi Takoradi (116,000)
Official language English
Ethnic composition Akan 44.0%; Moshi-
Dagomba 16.0%; Ewe 13.0%; Ga-Adangme
8.0%; European and others 19.0%

Religious affiliations indigenous beliefs
38%; Muslim 30%; Christian 24%; others 8%
Currency 1 new cedi (C) = 100 pesewas
Economy Gross national product (per capita
1993) US $430; Gross domestic product (1993)
US $6,084 million
Life expectancy at birth male 53.6 yr;
female 57.5 yr
Major resources cocoa, timber, gold, indus-
trial diamonds, manganese, bauxite, fisheries,
oil, natural gas, rubber
Major international organizations GATT,
IBRD, IMF, NAM, UN, UNESCO, UNPROFOR,
WHO

Ghana, formerly the Gold Coast, is on the west coast of central Africa, facing the Gulf of
Guinea. More than half the country is occupied by the Volta basin, a fertile low-lying and
frequently flooded area surrounding Lake Volta; much of the rest is tropical forest.
Agriculture is the mainstay of the economy, with cocoa and timber earning most export
revenue. Gold, diamonds, oil, and other minerals make a significant contribution.

GREECE

Land area 131,957 sq km (50,949 sq mi)
Major physical features highest point: Olympus 2,917 m (9,570 ft); longest river Vardar (part) 382 km (241 mi)
Population (1994) 10,564,630
Form of government multiparty republic with one legislative house
Largest cities Athens (capital – 3,097,000); Salonika (378,000); Patras (155,000)
Official language Greek
Ethnic composition Greek 98.0%; others 2.0%
Religious affiliations Greek Orthodox 97.6%; Muslim 1.5%; Roman Catholic 0.4%; Protestant 0.1%; others 0.4%
Currency 1 drachma (Dr) = 100 lepta
Economy Gross national product (per capita 1993) US $7,390; Gross domestic product (1993) US $63,240 million
Life expectancy at birth male 75.2 yr; female 80.3 yr
Major resources tourism, olives, citrus fruits, tobacco, bauxite, manganese, marble
Major international organizations EU, GATT, IBRD, IMF, NATO, UN, UNHCR, WHO

Greece is the ancient center of European culture. Some 2,000 islands account for one fifth of its landmass, making commercial shipping of central economic importance.

GRENADA

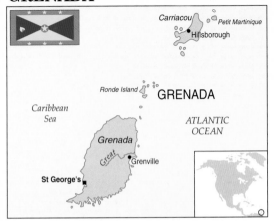

Land area 345 sq km (133 sq mi)

Major physical feature highest point: Mount St Catherine 840 m (2,756 ft)

Population (1994) 94,109

Form of government multiparty constitutional monarchy with two legislative houses

Capital city St George's (29,000)

Official language English

Ethnic composition black 84.0%; mixed 12.0%; Asian Indian 3.0%; white 1.0%

Religious affiliations Roman Catholic 64.4%; Anglican 20.7%; other Protestants 13.8%; others 1.1%

Currency 1 East Caribbean dollar = 100 cents

Economy Gross national product (per capita 1991) US $2,180

Life expectancy at birth male 68.0 yr; female 72.8 yr

Major resources cocoa, bananas, nutmeg and mace, timber, deepwater harbors, tourism

Major international organizations CARICOM, ECLAC, GATT, IBRD, IMF, LAES, UN, UNESCO, WHO

Grenada is a Caribbean island state in the lesser Antilles, off the coast of Venezuela. The main island, Grenada, is the most southerly of the volcanic Windward Islands, but the territory also includes the southernmost islands of the neighboring Grenadine group. The French colonized Grenada in 1650, it was seized by Britain in the 18th century, and became an independent republic in 1974, with a parliamentary democracy based on the British system. In 1979 the New Jewel Movement, led by Maurice Bishop, seized power in a left-wing coup, but in 1983 he was deposed and murdered by rival Marxists. The United States forces invaded to restore constitutional government. Grenada's economy is almost completely dependent on tourism and export revenues from cash crops.

GUATEMALA

Land area 108,889 sq km (42,042 sq mi)

Major physical features highest point: Tajumulco 4,220 m (13,845 ft); longest river: Motagua 550 km (340 mi)

Population (1994) 10,721,387

Form of government multiparty republic with one legislative house

Largest cities Guatemala City (capital – 2,000,000); Puerto Barrios (338,000)

Official language Spanish

Ethnic composition Ladino 56.0% (mestizo – mixed Indian and European ancestry); Indian 44.0%

Religious affiliations Roman Catholic 75.0%; Protestant 25.0%

Currency 1 quetzal = 100 centavos

Economy Gross national product (per capita 1993) US $1,100; Gross domestic product (1993) US $11,309 million

Life expectancy at birth male 61.9 yr; female 67.1 yr

Major resources coffee, sugar, bananas, cardamon, beef, rare woods, fish, chicle

Major international organizations BCIE, ECLAC, GATT, IBRD, IMF, LAES, NAM, UN, UNESCO, WHO

Guatemala is a mountainous volcanic country in Central America, southwest of Mexico. The economy is supported by cash crops of coffee, sugar, bananas, timber and chicle.

GUINEA

Land area 245,857 sq km (94,926 sq mi)
Major physical features highest point: Mount Nimba 1,752 m (5,748 ft); longest river: Niger (part) 4,200 km (2,600 mi)
Population (1994) 6,391,536
Form of government republic with military government
Largest cities Conakry (capital – 705,000); Kankan (88,800)
Official language French
Ethnic composition Peuhl 40%; Malinke 30%; Sousson 20%; indigenous tribes 10%

Religious affiliations Muslim 85.0%; traditional beliefs 5.0%; Christian 1.5%; others 8.5%
Currency 1 Guinean franc = 100 centimes
Economy Gross national product (per capita 1993) US $500; Gross domestic product (1993) US $3,172 million
Life expectancy at birth male 41.9 yr; female 46.4 yr
Major resources bauxite, coffee, tropical fruit, fish, uranium, timber, diamonds, gold
Major international organizations IBRD, IMF, NAM, OIC, UN, UNECSO, WHO

Guinea lies on the west coast of Africa, surrounded by six other African nations. Apart from the low-lying areas of savanna grassland around the rivers and the coast, Guinea is mountainous and covered with dense tropical rainforest. It was colonized by the French in the 19th century, and achieved independence in 1958 as the People's Revolutionary Republic of Guinea. The economy depends on mining and processing the country's considerable reserves of bauxite, and on cash crops of coffee and fruit.

GUINEA-BISSAU

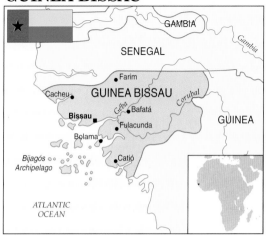

Land area 36,125 sq km (13,948 sq mi)
Population (1994) 1,098,231
Form of government one-party republic with one legislative house
Capital city Bissau (125,000)
Official language Portuguese
Ethnic composition African 99.0% (Balanta 30.0%; Fula 20.0%; Manjaca 14.0%; Mandinga 13.0%; Papel 7.0%); European and Mulatto 1.0%
Religious affiliations traditional beliefs 65.0%; Muslim 30%; Christian 5.0%

Currency 1 Guinea-Bissau peso = 100 centavos
Economy Gross national product (per capita 1993) US $240; Gross domestic product (1993) US $241 million
Life expectancy at birth male 45.8 yr; female 49.1 yr
Major resources ground nuts (peanuts), cashew nuts, coconuts, cotton, fish, timber
Major international organizations IMF, NAM, OIC, UN, UNESCO, WHO

Guinea-Bissau, formerly Portuguese Guinea, lies on the west coast of Africa between Senegal and Guinea. The territory also includes the neighboring islands of the Bijagós Archipelago. It is a country of plains, broad estuaries and swamplands, rich in river wildlife that includes flamingoes, crocodiles and pelicans. Guinea-Bissau was colonized just as the Portuguese slave trade began to decline in the 19th century. It won its independence in 1974, and is currently ruled by a one-party military government. The state-run economy is based on agriculture, but recent plagues of locusts and periodic drought have made much of the country dependent on foreign aid. Known reserves of petroleum are, as yet, unexploited.

GUYANA

Land area 215,083 sq km (83,044 sq mi)
Major physical features highest point:
Roraima 2,810 m (9,216 ft); longest river:
Essequibo 1,040 km (630 mi)
Population (1994) 729,425
Form of government multiparty republic
with one legislative house
Capital city Georgetown (188,000)
Official language English
Ethnic composition Asian Indian 51.4%;
black 30.5%; mixed 11.0%; Amerindian 5.3%;
Chinese 0.2%; white 0.1%; others 1.5%

Religious affiliations Christian 57.0%;
Hindu 33.0%; Muslim 9.0%; others 1.0%
Currency 1 Guyana dollar (G$) = 100 cents
Economy Gross national product (per capita
1993) US $290
Life expectancy at birth male 66.7 yr;
female 68.3 yr
Major resources bauxite, sugar, coconuts,
rice, shrimp, timber, gold, diamonds
Major international organizations
CARICOM, GATT, IMF, LAES, NAM, UN,
UNESCO, WHO

Guyana, formerly British Guyana, is a small state on the north coast of South America.
Its name is derived from the Amerindian term "land of waters". Most of the terrain is a
thickly forested plateau, with coastal plains developed for agriculture. Guyana has
extremely rich deposits of bauxite – exporting and processing this valuable mineral
dominates the economy and accounts for most of its export revenue. Sugar, coconuts
and rice are important cash crops, and there are also small deposits of diamonds.

HAITI

Land area 27,400 sq km (10,569 sq mi)
Population (1994) 6,491,450
Form of government multiparty republic with two legislative houses
Capital city Port-au-Prince (1,144,000)
Official languages Haitian Creole, French
Ethnic composition black 95.0%; mulatto 4.9%; white 0.1%
Official language French
Religious affiliations Roman Catholic 80.3%; Protestant 15.8%; others 3.9% (voodoo is practiced by many local people)
Currency 1 gourde (G) = 100 centimes
Economy Gross national product (per capita 1993) US $370
Life expectancy at birth male 43.4 yr; female 46.8 yr
Major resources coffee, sugar cane, bauxite
Major international organizations GATT, IBRD, IMF, LAES, UN, UNESCO, WHO

Haiti occupies the western third of the island of Hispaniola in the central Caribbean, east of Cuba. The rest of Hispaniola is occupied by the Dominican Republic. Haiti was a French colony in the 17th century, when African slaves worked the sugar and coffee plantations. Most of the inhabitants today are the Creole descendants of slaves, French speaking, and practicing a mixture of Roman Catholicism and voodoo beliefs. The colonial power was driven out in the 19th century, but in the following decades a number of brutal dictators ruled the country. In 1957 Francois "Papa Doc" Duvalier established a police state, and his son "Baby Doc" was deposed by a coup in 1986. Political instability continues, and the current head of state, Aristide, has spent time in enforced exile.

HONDURAS

Land area 112,088 sq km (43,277 sq mi)
Major physical features highest point:
Cerro Las Minas 2,827 m (9,275 ft); longest
river: Coco (part) 685 km (425 mi)
Population (1994) 5,314,794
Form of government multiparty republic
with one legislative house
Largest cities Tegucigalpa (capital –
679,000); San Pedro Sula (461,000)
Official language Spanish
Ethnic composition mestizo 89.9%;
Amerindian 6.7%; black 2.1%; white 1.3%

Religious affiliations Roman Catholic
97.0%; others 3.0%
Currency 1 lempira = 100 centavos
Economy Gross national product (per capita
1993) US $600; Gross domestic product (1993)
US $2,867 million
Life expectancy at birth male 65.2 yr;
female 70.1 yr
Major resources bananas, coffee, shellfish,
timber, gold, silver, copper, lead
Major international organizations ECLAC,
GATT, IBRD, IMF, LAES, UN, UNESCO, WHO

Honduras is a mountainous state on the Central American isthmus, with a long
Caribbean shoreline on the eastern coast, tapering to a much shorter shoreline on the
western Pacific coast. It was colonized by the Spanish in the 16th century, gained
independence from Spain as part of Mexico in 1821, and achieved complete autonomy in
1838. Almost two thirds of the population are farmers, and cash crops (chiefly bananas
and coffee) earn export revenue, though staple crops of maize, beans and rice scarcely
feed the population, and malnutrition is widespread. There are significant deposits of
precious minerals, but most remain unexploited. Repayments on foreign loans are
cripplingly high, and education, healthcare, and other public services are minimal.

HUNGARY

Land area 93,031 sq km (35,919 sq mi)
Major physical features highest point: Kékes 1,015 m (3,330 ft); longest river: Danube (part) 2,850 km (1,770 mi); largest lake: Lake Balaton 590 sq km (230 sq mi)
Population (1994) 10,319,113
Form of government multiparty republic with one legislative house
Capital city Budapest (2,016,000)
Official language Hungarian
Ethnic composition Hungarian 89.9%; gypsy 4.0%; German 2.6%; Serb 2.0%; Slovak 0.8%; Romanian 0.7%

Religious affiliations Roman Catholic 62.4%; Protestant 23.4%; nonreligious 12.9%; Jewish 0.8%; Eastern Orthodox 0.5%
Currency 1 forint (Ft) = 100 filler
Economy Gross national product (per capita 1993) US $3,350; Gross domestic product (1993) US $38,099 million
Life expectancy at birth male 67.4 yr; female 75.6 yr
Major resources bauxite, lignite, natural gas, grapes (for wine), cereals, timber
Major international organizations GATT, IBRD, IMF, UN, UNESCO, UNHCR, WHO

Hungary is a landlocked state in Eastern Europe, much of it low-lying fertile farmland in the Danube basin, which extends eastward into the "Great Hungarian Plain". Since the breakup of the eastern communist bloc, following the dissolution of the Soviet Union in 1991, Hungary has been making the transition to a free-market economy. Manufacturing industry (chemicals, engineering and transportation equipment) is undergoing a massive program of privatization, and trade with the European Community is flourishing.

ICELAND

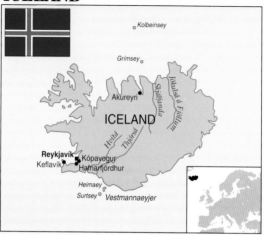

Land area 103,000 sq km (39,768 sq mi)
Major physical features highest point: Hvannadalshnúkur 2,119 m (6,951 ft); longest river: Thjórsá 230 km (143 mi)
Population (1994) 263,599
Form of government multiparty republic with two legislative houses
Capital city Reykjavik (143,000)
Official language Icelandic
Ethnic composition Icelandic 96.3%; other Scandinavians 1.3%; American 0.5%; others 1.9%
Official religion Lutheranism

Religious affiliations Lutheran 96.2%; non-religious 1.3%; Roman Catholic 0.9%; other Christians 0.6%; others 1.0%
Currency 1 Icelandic króna = 100 aurar
Economy Gross national product (per capita 1993) US $22,580
Life expectancy at birth male 76.6 yr; female 81.2 yr
Major resources fisheries, hydropower, geo-thermal power, diatomite
Major international organizations GATT, IBRD, IMF, NATO, UN, UNESCO, WHO

Iceland is an island republic just south of the Arctic Circle. It provides a harsh volcanically active habitat for its people, who are direct descendants of the original 9th-century Viking settlers. Earth tremors are frequent, and hot springs in volcanic areas provide much of the country's hot water and heating. Fishing is the cornerstone of the economy; much of the fishing fleet is government owned, and fish products account for three-quarters of national exports. In recent years, however, depletion of fish stocks has made necessary a system of quotas and bans, and managed fish farms are becoming more popular. Vegetables and flowers are cultivated in greenhouses heated by geothermal power.

INDIA

India occupies most of the Indian subcontinent, bordering Pakistan to the west, China, Nepal and Bhutan to the north, and Bangladesh and Myanmar (Burma) to the east. The country boasts one of the world's oldest civilizations (the Aryans) whose history has been recorded as far back as the 15th century BC. Today India is made up of a rich diversity of races, speaking over 700 different languages and dialects. Fifteen of these languages have official status, but Hindi is used as a first or second language by more than four-fifths of the population. Since winning independence from Britain in 1947, India has had troubled relations with its neighbors, flaring into war with Pakistan in 1965. Gross national product remains one of the lowest in the world. Imports have continued to outweigh exports, while foreign aid is declining and foreign debts continue to mount.

Land area 3,287,263 sq km (1,269,219 sq mi)
Major physical features highest point: Kanchenjunga 8,598 m (28,208 ft); longest rivers: Brahmaputra (part) 2,900 km (1,800 mi); Ganges 2,506 km (1,557 mi)
Population (1994) 919,903,056
Form of government federal multiparty republic with two legislative houses
Largest cities Bombay (12,572,000); Calcutta (10,916,000); New Delhi (capital – 8,375,000); Madras (5,361,000); Hyderabad (4,280,000); Bangalore (4,087,000); Ahmadabad (3,298,000)
Official languages Hindi; Bengali; Telugu; Marathi; Tamil; Urdu; Gujarati; Malayalami; Kannada; Oriya; Punjabi; Assamese; Kashmiri; Sindhi; Sanskrit

Ethnic composition Indo-Aryan 72%; Dravidian 25%; Mongoloid and others 3%
Religious affiliations Hindu 80.0%; Muslim 14.0%; Christian 2.4%; Sikh 2.0%; Buddhist 0.7%; Jain 0.5%; others 0.4%
Currency 1 Indian rupee = 100 paisa
Economy Gross national product (per capita 1993) US $300; Gross domestic product (1993) US $225,431 million
Life expectancy at birth male 58.1 yr; female 59.1 yr
Major resources coal, iron ore, manganese, mica, bauxite, titanium ore, chromite, natural gas, diamonds, petroleum, limestone
Major international organizations ESCAP, GATT, IBRD, IMF, NAM, UN, UNESCO, UNPROFOR, WHO

States of the Republic

(with populations for 1991)

Andhra Pradesh	(66,508,008)	**Manipur**	(1,837,149)
Arunachal Pradesh	(864,558)	**Meghalaya**	(1,774,778)
Assam	(22,414,322)	**Mizoram**	(689,756)
Bihar	(86,374,465)	**Nagaland**	(1,209,546
Goa	(1,169,793)	**Orissa**	(31,659,736)
Gujarat	(41,309,582)	**Punjab**	(20,281,969)
Haryana	(16,463,648)	**Rajasthan**	(44,005,990)
Himachal Pradesh	(5,170,877)	**Sikkim**	(406,457)
Jammu & Kashmir	(7,718,700)	**Tamil Nadu**	(55,858,946)
Karnataka	(44,977,201)	**Tripura**	(2,757,205)
Kerala	(29,098,518)	**Uttar Pradesh**	(139,112,287)
Madhya Pradesh	(66,181,170)	**West Bengal**	(68,077,965)
Maharashtra	(78,937,187)		

JAMMU
AND KASHMIR

HIMACHAL
PRADESH

PUNJAB   CHANDIGARH

HARYANA

DELHI

New Delhi

ARUNACHAL
PRADESH

SIKKIM

ASSAM   NAGALAND

UTTAR
PRADESH

RAJASTHAN

MEGHALAYA

MANIPUR

BIHAR

TRIPURA   MIZORAM

WEST
BENGAL

GUJARAT

MADYHA PRADESH

INDIA

DAMAN
& DIU

ORISSA

MAHARASHTRA

DADRA &
NAGAR HAVELI

ANDHRA
PRADESH   to Pondicherry

GOA

KARNATAKA

LAKSHADWEEP
to
Pondicherry

PONDICHERRY

TAMIL
NADU   to Pondicherry

KERALA

ANDAMAN AND
NICOBAR
ISLANDS

INDONESIA

Land area 1,919,443 sq km (741,101 sq mi)
Major physical features highest point:
Mount Jaya (New Guinea) 5,029 m
(16,499 ft); longest river: Barito (Borneo)
885 km (550 mi); largest lake: Lake Toba
(Sumatra) 1,775 sq km (685 sq mi)
Population (1994) 200,409,741
Form of government multiparty republic
with two legislative houses
Largest cities Jakarta (capital – 7,886,000);
Surabaya (2,224,000); Medan (1,806,000);
Bandung (1,567,000)
Official language Bahasa Indonesian
Ethnic composition Javanese 45.0%;

Sundanese 14.0%; Madurese 7.5%; Coastal
Malays 7.5%; others 26.0%
Religious affiliations Muslim 86.9%; Christian
9.6%; Hindu 1.9%; Buddhist 1.0%; others 0.6%
Currency the rupiah
Economy Gross national product (per capita
1993) US $740; Gross domestic product (1993)
US $144,707 million
Life expectancy at birth male 58.7 yr;
female 62.9 yr
Major resources petroleum, tin, natural
gas, nickel, timber, bauxite, copper, gold, fish
Major international organizations GATT,
IBRD, IMF, NAM, OPEC, UN, UNESCO, WHO

Indonesia is a vast archipelago of 13,677 islands forming a bridge between Asia and
Australasia that reaches from Sumatra in the west to Irian Jaya in the east. The two
largest islands in the archipelago are shared with other countries: the northern coastal
section of Borneo belongs to Malaysia; while the eastern half of New Guinea forms the
main part of Papua New Guinea. Indonesia is extremely rich in mineral resources, yet
with a large and rapidly increasing population, it remains a relatively poor country.

IRAN

Land area 1,643,503 sq km (634,559 sq mi)
Major physical features highest point:
Damavand 5,671 m (18,606 ft); longest river:
Karun 850 km (528 mi)
Population (1994) 65,615,474
Form of government one-party republic
Largest cities Tehran (capital 6,476,000);
Mashhad (1,759,000); Esfahan (1,127,000)
Official language Farsi (Persian)
Ethnic composition Persian 45.6%;
Azerbaijani 16.8%; Kurdish 9.1%; Gilaki 5.3%;
Luri 4.3%; Mazandarani 3.6%; Baluchi 2.3%;
Arab 2.2%; others 10.8%

Official religion Islam
Religious affiliations Shi'ite Muslim 95%;
Sunni Muslim 4%; Christian, Jewish & others 1%
Currency 1 Iranian rial (Rl) = 100 tomans
Economy Gross national product (per capita
1993) US $1,648; Gross domestic product
(1993) US $107,335 million
Life expectancy at birth male 64.7 yr;
female 66.7 yr
Major resources petroleum, natural gas,
fruits, nuts, hides, coal, chromium, copper
Major international organizations IBRD,
IMF, NAM, OPEC, UN, UNESCO, UNHCR, WHO

Iran is one of the largest of the Gulf states, sharing frontiers with seven other Asian
countries, and with access to the Persian Gulf and the Caspian Sea. Much of the country
is a massive semi-arid plateau, home to the ancient Persian civilizations, with a cultural
heritage stretching back more than 5,000 years. The economy is almost totally dependent
on petroleum, but since 1980 prosperity has been severely damaged by war with Iraq.

IRAQ

Land area 438,317 sq km (169,235 sq mi)

Major physical features highest point: Huji Ibrahim 3,600 m (11,811 ft); longest river; Euphrates (part) 2,720 km (1,700 mi)

Population (1994) 19,889,666

Form of government multiparty republic with one legislative house

Largest cities Baghdad (capital – 4,649,000); Basra (617,000); Mosul (571,000)

Official language Arabic

Ethnic composition Arab 77.1%; Kurdish 19.0%; Turkmen 1.4%; Persian 0.8%; Assyrian 0.8%; others 0.9%

Official religion Islam

Religious affiliations Shi'ite Muslim 60–65%; Sunni Muslim 32–37%; Christian or others 3.0%

Currency 1 Iraqi dinar (ID) = 200 dirhams

Economy Gross national product (per capita 1991) US $2,000

Life expectancy at birth male 64.9 yr; female 66.7 yr

Major resources petroleum, natural gas, phosphates, sulfur

Major international organizations IBRD, IMF, NAM, OAPEC, OPEC, UN, UNESCO, WHO

Iraq is an Arab republic at the northwestern end of the Persian Gulf. The terrain ranges from mountainous in the northeast, to the fertile basin of the Tigris and Euphrates in the center (formerly Mesopotamia), to desert in the southwest. Petroleum is the mainstay of the economy, but war with Iran from 1980, and against a US-led international force resisting the invasion of Kuwait 1990–91, left the economy crippled with debt.

IRELAND

Land area   70,285 sq km (27,137 sq mi)
Major physical features   highest point: Carrauntoohill (Macgillicuddy's Reeks) 1,041 m (3,414 ft); longest river: Shannon 370 km (230 mi)
Population   (1994) 3,539,296
Form of government   multiparty republic with two legislative houses
Largest cities   Dublin (capital – 1,024,000); Cork (174,000); Limerick (75,000); Galway (51,000); Waterford (42,000)
Official languages   Irish, English
Ethnic composition   Irish 93.0%; others 7.0%

Religious affiliations   Roman Catholic 93.0%; Church of Ireland 3.0%; Presbyterian 0.4%; others 3.6%
Currency   1 Irish pound (Ir £) = 100 pence
Economy   Gross national product (per capita 1993) US $13,000; Gross domestic product (1993) US $42,962 million
Life expectancy at birth   male 72.8 yr; female 78.7 yr
Major resources   natural gas, peat, dairy products, tourism, fisheries, zinc
Major international organizations   EU, GATT, IBRD, IMF, UN, UNESCO, UNPROFOR, WHO

The Republic of Ireland occupies some five sixths of the island of Ireland, about 80 km (50 mi) off the west coast of Britain. A broken rim of mountains on the circumference surrounds a low-lying center, much of which is fertile farmland. Manufacturing and services account for the largest sector of the economy, with beer, whiskey, Irish glass, textiles, and food products being exported throughout the EC and the United States.

113

ISRAEL

Land area 20,700 sq km (7,992 sq mi)
Major physical features highest point:
Mount Meron 1,208 m (3,963 ft); lowest point:
Dead Sea –400 m (–1,312 ft); longest river:
Jordan (part) 320 km (200 mi)
Population (1994) 5,050,850
Form of government multiparty republic
with one legislative house
Largest cities Jerusalem (capital –
495,000); Tel Aviv-Jaffa (318,000)
Official languages Hebrew, Arabic
Ethnic composition Jewish 83.0%; Arab and
others 17.0%

Religious affiliations Jewish 83.0%; Muslim
14.0%; Christian 2.0%; Druze and others 1.0%
Currency 1 new Israeli sheqel = 100 agorot
Economy Gross national product (per capita
1993) US $13,920; Gross domestic product
(1993) US $69,739 million
Life expectancy at birth male 75.9 yr;
female 80.2 yr
Major resources fruits and vegetables,
copper, phosphates, bromide, potash
Major international organizations GATT,
IBRD, IMF, UN, UNESCO, UNHCR, WHO

The small state of Israel was established as a Jewish homeland in Palestine in 1948. Its
people claim historic ties with that area going back more than 3,000 years, but the
Palestinian Arabs, whose claim is no less ancient, dispute Jewish territorial rights, and
Israel exists in an uneasy truce with its Arab neighbors. Its capital, Jerusalem, is also a
holy city for the Christian and Muslim faiths.

ITALY

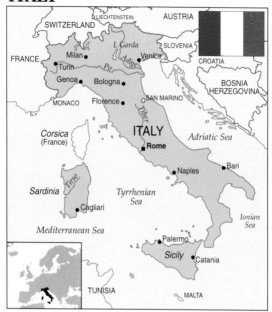

Land area 301,277 sq km (116,324 sq mi)
Major physical features highest point: Monte Rosa 4,634 m (15,203 ft); longest river: Po 620 km (380 mi)
Population (1994) 58,138,394
Form of government multiparty republic with two legislative houses
Largest cities Rome (capital – 2,791,000); Milan (1,432,000); Naples (1,206,000)
Official language Italian
Ethnic composition Italian 94.1%; Sardinian 2.7%; Rhaetian 1.3%; others 1.9%

Religious affiliations Roman Catholic 83.2%; nonreligious 16.2%; others 0.6%
Currency 1 lira (Lit) = 100 centesimi
Economy Gross national product (per capita 1993) US $19,840; Gross domestic product (1993) US $991,386 million
Life expectancy at birth male 74.4 yr; female 81.0 yr
Major resources fruit, olives, grapes (for wine), cheese, tourism, fisheries, marble
Major international organizations EU, G-7, GATT, IBRD, IMF, NATO, UN, UNHCR, WHO

Italy is Europe's youngest unified state, and each region has a long, rich cultural history. Its exports of fruit, olives and wine, are prized, and manufacturing industry is booming.

IVORY COAST

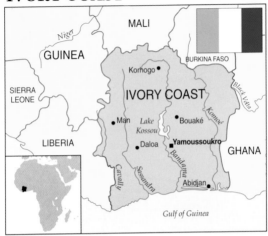

Land area 320,763 sq km (123,847 sq mi)
Major physical feature highest point: Mount Nimba 1,752 m (5,748 ft)
Population (1994) 13,500,000
Form of government multiparty republic with one legislative house
Largest cities Abidjan (2,534,000); Bouaké (390,000); Yamoussoukro (capital – 120,000)
Official language French
Ethnic composition Akan 41.4%; Kru 16.7%; Voltaic 15.7%; Malinke 14.9%; Southern Mande 10.2%; others 1.1%

Religious affiliations traditional beliefs 60%; Muslim 20%; Roman Catholic 15%; Protestant 5%
Currency 1 CFA franc = 100 centimes
Economy Gross national product (per capita 1993) US $630; Gross domestic product (1993) US $8,087 million
Life expectancy at birth male 53.0 yr; female 56.0 yr
Major resources cocoa, coffee, bananas, palm oil, timber, petroleum, cotton, diamonds,
Major international organizations GATT, IBRD, IMF, NAM, UN, UNESCO, WHO

The Ivory Coast faces the Gulf of Guinea on the west coast of Africa. The lagoons and sandbars of the coast rise gently into a deep band of tropical rainforest. The rainforest is a valuable source of hardwoods for export, and large areas have been cleared for plantations, yielding cash crops of coffee and cocoa. The thinly populated northern plateau is covered in savanna grasslands, rising to the northern highlands and Mount Nimba in the northwest. The economy depends on cash crops, timber and fish, and there are small but valuable deposits of offshore oil, diamonds and other minerals. A worldwide slump in coffee and cocoa prices in the mid-1980s caused a deep recession.

JAMAICA

Land area 10,991 sq km (4,244 sq mi)

Major physical feature highest point: Blue Mountain Peak 2,256 m (7,402 ft)

Population (1990) 2,555,064

Form of government multiparty constitutional monarchy with two legislative houses

Capital city Kingston (588,000)

Official language English

Ethnic composition black 76.3%; Afro-European 15.1%; Amerindian/Afro-Indian 3.4%; white 3.2%; others 2.0%

Religious affiliations Protestant 55.9%; Roman Catholic 5.0%; nonreligious 17.7%; others 10.2%; not stated 11.2%

Currency 1 Jamaican dollar = 100 cents

Economy Gross national product (per capita 1993) US $1,440; Gross domestic product (1993) $3,825 million

Life expectancy at birth male 72.2 yr; female 76.7 yr

Major resources sugar, tourism, bananas, rum, coffee, cocoa, tropical fruit, bauxite

Major international organizations CARICOM, GATT, IBRD, IMF, LAES, UN, WHO

The lush, tropical island of Jamaica lies in the Caribbean, south of Cuba and west of Haiti. The island's original Arawak peoples were wiped out by the Spanish settlers who came to the region in the wake of Columbus. African slaves were imported by the colonists to work the land, and the inhabitants today are their direct descendants. In 1655 the British captured Jamaica and, in time, its slave-worked sugar plantations became an immensely profitable part of the British Empire. This prosperity ended in 1833 with the abolition of slavery, when banana growing was introduced to replace some of the sugar plantations. Jamaica gained full independence in 1962, but remained within the Commonwealth. Today tourism is the chief source of revenue.

JAPAN

Land area   377,815 sq km (145,875 sq mi)
Major physical features   highest point:
Mount Fuji 3,776 m (12,388 ft)
Population   (1994) 125,106,937
Form of government   multiparty constitutional monarchy with two legislative houses
Capital city   Tokyo (11,936,000)
Official language   Japanese
Ethnic composition   Japanese 99.2%;
Korean 0.6%; others 0.2%

Religious affiliations   Most Japanese are
adherents both of Shinto (93.1%) and
Buddhism (73.9%); Christian 1.4%
Currency   Yen (¥)
Economy   Gross national product (per capita
1993) US $31,490; Gross domestic product
(1993) US $117,587 million
Life expectancy at birth   male 76.5 yr;
female 82.3 yr
Major resources   manufacturing & finance

Japan is an archipelago of some 4,000 islands lying across a fault line off the eastern coast of mainland Asia. The country's geographic isolation, and the fact that it chose to cut itself off from other cultures for centuries, has formed a very distinctive and uniform society with a powerful work ethic for the good of the whole. It has one of the lowest crime rates in the world. Since World War II, Japan has transformed itself from an isolated feudal society into one of the world's most dynamic industrial nations, at the same time building the world's strongest economy. This has been achieved in spite of the fact that the country has almost no natural resources and must import raw materials and fuel for energy. Japan is a constitutional monarchy with the emperor as head of state.

Prefectures

(with population for 1993)

Hokkaidō
  Hokkaidō (5,666,000)

Honshū
Aichi	(6,795,000)
Akita	(1,216,000)
Aomori	(1,470,000)
Chiba	(5,721,000)
Fukui	(825,000)
Fukushima	(2,122,000)
Gifu	(2,085,000)
Gumma	(1,988,000)
Hiroshima	(2,872,000)
Hyōgo	(5,490,000)
Ibaraki	(2,916,000)
Ishikawa	(1,171,000)
Iwate	(1,415,000)
Kanagawa	(8,149,000)
Kyōto	(2,605,000)
Mie	(1,818,000)
Miyagi	(2,290,000)
Nagano	(2,170,000)
Nara	(1,413,000)
Niigata	(2,478,000)
Okayama	(1,936,000)
Ōsaka	(8,723,000)
Saitama	(6,632,000)
Shiga	(1,258,000)
Shimane	(772,000)
Shizuoka	(3,712,000)
Tochigi	(1,966,000)
Tokyo	(11,830,000)
Tottori	(615,000)
Toyama	(1,121,000)
Wakayama	(1,079,000)
Yamagata	(1,253,000)
Yamaguchi	(1,562,000)
Yamanashi	(865,000)

Kyushū
Fukuoka	(4,875,000)
Kagoshima	(1,786,000)
Kumamoto	(1,847,000)
Miyazaki	(1,170,000)
Nagasaki	(1,550,000)
Ōita	(1,232,000)
Saga	(879,000)

Ryukyu Island
  Okinawa (1,247,000)

Shikoku
Ehime	(1,509,000)
Kagawa	(1,025,000)
Kōchi	(815,000)
Tokushima	(830,000)

K.	KANAGAWA
KUM.	KUMAMOTO
KY.	KYŌTO
N.	NARA
OK.	OKAYAMA
OS.	ŌSAKA
S.	SHIGA
T.	TOKYO
TOK.	TOKUSHIMA
W.	WAKAYAMA
Y.	YAMANASHI

JORDAN

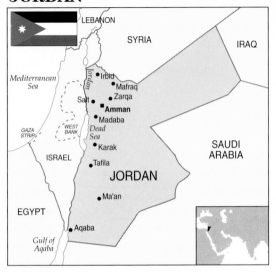

Land area 89,206 sq km (34,443 sq mi)
Major physical features highest point: Jebel Ram 1,754 m (5,755 ft); lowest point: Dead Sea –400 m (–1,312 ft); longest river: Jordan (part) 320 km (200 mi)
Population (1994) 3,961,194
Form of government constitutional monarchy with two legislative houses
Largest cities Amman (capital – 1,160,000); Irbid (680,000); Zarqa (405,000)
Official language Arabic
Ethnic composition Arab 99.2%; Circassian 0.5%; Armenian 0.1%; Turkish 0.1%; Kurdish 0.1%

Official religion Islam
Religious affiliations Sunni Muslim 93.0%; Christian 4.9%; others 2.1%
Currency 1 Jordanian dinar = 1,000 fils
Economy Gross national product (per capita 1993) US $1,190; Gross domestic product (1993) US $4,441 million
Life expectancy at birth male 70.0 yr; female 73.8 yr
Major resources phosphates, potash, shale oil, fruit, tourism
Major international organizations IBRD, IMF, LORCS, NAM, UN, UNPROFOR, WHO

The small Arab kingdom of Jordan shares a western frontier with its political rival Israel, and has access to the Red Sea and beyond through a short coastline on the Gulf of Aqaba. Jordan is heavily dependent on foreign grants and loans, but the recent discovery of reserves of phosphates and potash has boosted the economy. However, an influx of Palestinian refugees from the West Bank has stretched reserves to the limit.

KAZAKHSTAN

Land area 2,717,300 sq km (1,049,200 sq mi)
Major physical features highest point:
Khan-Tengri 6,398 m (20,991 ft); lowest point:
Mangyshlak Depression −132 m (−433 ft);
longest river: Irtysh (part) 4,400 km (2,760 mi)
Population (1994) 17,267,554
Form of government multiparty republic
with one legislative house
Largest cities Alma-Ata (capital –
1,147,000); Karaganda (613,000); Chimkent
(438,000); Semipalatinsk (339,000)
Official language Kazakh
Ethnic composition Kazakh 42%; Russian

38%; Ukrainian 5.4%; Tatar 2%; others 12.6%
Religious affiliations Muslim 47%; Russian
Orthodox 44%; Protestant 2.0%; others 7.0%
Currency the tenge (from November 1993)
Economy Gross national product (per capita
1993) US $1,560; Gross domestic product
(1993) US $24,728 million
Life expectancy at birth male 63.4 yr;
female 72.9 yr
Major resources petroleum, coal, iron ore,
bauxite, manganese, nickel, cobalt, copper
Major international organizations CIS,
IBRD, IMF, UN, UNESCO, WHO

Kazakhstan is the second largest (after Russia) of the republics that made up the
former Soviet Union. The country is named after the Kazakh people, Turkic-speaking
nomads who sustained a powerful Khanate in the region before Russian domination.
Kazakhstan has huge mineral wealth, and a strong manufacturing base, though pollution
is a problem. The agricultural sector is also extremely productive.

KENYA

Land area 571,416 sq km (220,625 sq mi)
Major physical features highest point: Mount Kenya 5,200 m (17,060 ft)
Population (1994) 28,240,658
Form of government one-party republic
Largest cities Nairobi (capital 1,429,000); Mombasa (457,000); Kisumu (198,000)
Official languages Swahili, English
Ethnic composition Kikuyu 20.9%; Luhya 13.8%; Luo 12.8%; Kemba 11.3%; Kalenjiu 10.8%; other Africans 29.2%; Asian 0.6%; European 0.3%; Arab 0.3%
Religious affiliations Protestant 26.5%; Roman Catholic 26.4%; traditional beliefs 18.9%; African Christian 17.6%; Muslim 6.0%; Orthodox 2.5%; others 2.1%
Currency 1 Kenyan shilling = 100 cents
Economy Gross national product (per capita 1993) US $270; Gross domestic product (1993) US $4,691 million
Life expectancy at birth male 51.5 yr; female 55.0 yr
Major resources tea, coffee, gold, limestone, rubies, garnets, tourism
Major international organizations GATT, IBRD, IMF, UN, UNESCO, UNPROFOR, WHO

Kenya lies across the equator on the eastern coast of Africa. Large areas of the country have been developed as game reserves, and tourism is increasing, encouraged by the government. Cash crops of tea and coffee still account for most export revenue.

KIRIBATI

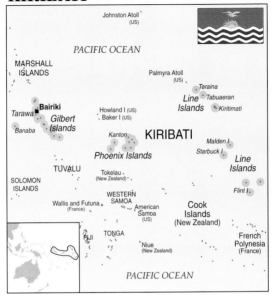

Land area 849 sq km (328 sq mi)

Major physical features largest island:
Kiritimati (Line Is) 388 sq km (150 sq mi);
highest point: Banaba 81 m (266 ft)

Population (1994) 77,000

Form of government nonparty republic with
one legislative house

Capital city Bairiki (Tarawa atoll,
population 24,000)

Official language English

Ethnic composition I-Kiribati 97.4%; mixed
(I-Kiribati/others) 1.5%; Tuvaluan 0.5%;
Europeans 0.2%; others 0.4%

Religious affiliations Roman Catholic
53.5%; Kiribati Protestant (Congregational)
39.1%; Baha'i 2.4%; others 5.0%

Currency 1 Australian dollar = 100 cents

Economy Gross national product (per capita
1993) US $750

Life expectancy at birth male 52.6 yr;
female 55.8 yr

Major resources copra, seaweed, fish

Major international organizations IBRD,
IMF, UNESCO, WHO

Kiribati is made up of three widely separated archipelagoes spread across a vast area of
the Pacific. The islands were rich in phosphates, but exploitation for export had
exhausted the resource by the late 1970s. Copra and fish are the chief exports today.

KUWAIT

Land area   17,818 sq km (6,880 sq mi)
Major physical feature   highest point: ash-Shaqaya 290 m (951 ft)
Population   (1994) 1,819,322
Form of government   nonparty constitutional monarchy with one legislative house
Capital city   Kuwait (189,000)
Official language   Arabic
Ethnic composition   Kuwaiti 45.0%; other Arab 35.0%; South Asian 9.0%; Iranian 4.0%; others 7.0%
Official religion   Islam

Religious affiliations   Sunni Muslim 63%; Shi'ite Muslim 27%; Christian 8%; Hindu 2%
Currency   1 Kuwaiti dinar (KD) = 1,000 fils
Economy   Gross national product (per capita 1993) US $19,360; Gross domestic product (1993) US $22,402 million
Life expectancy at birth   male 72.8 yr; female 77.3 yr
Major resources   petroleum, natural gas, fish
Major international organizations   GATT, IMF, OAPEC, OPEC, UN, UNESCO, WHO

Kuwait is an independent Arab Emirate at the northwestern tip of the Persian Gulf. The discovery of oil in the region during the 1930s brought it unexpected prosperity, and the oil industry continues to be the mainstay of the economy today. In 1990 Kuwait was invaded by its neighbor Iraq, intending to capture the country's rich oil fields. Sovereignty was only regained after the intervention of western forces who took part in a bitter war, in which both countries suffered considerable losses and environmental damage. Wildlife includes various desert and shoreline species, but numbers were severely depleted as a result of oil pollution during the Gulf war.

KYRGYZSTAN

Land area 198,500 sq km (76,600 sq mi)
Major physical features highest point: Pobedy Peak 7,439 m (24,406 ft); longest river: Syr Darya (part) 2,200 km (1,370 mi)
Population (1994) 4,600,000
Form of government multiparty republic with one legislative house
Capital city Bishkek (625,000)
Official language Kirghizian
Ethnic composition Kirghiz 52.4%; Russian 21.5%; Uzbek 12.9%; Ukrainian 2.5%; Tatar 1.6%; others 9.1%

Religious affiliations Sunni Muslim with a Christian minority
Currency the som (since 1993)
Economy Gross national product (per capita 1993) US $850; Gross domestic product (1993) US $3,915 million
Life expectancy at birth male 65.0 yr; female 73.0 yr
Major resources livestock (cattle, sheep, goats), coal, oil, natural gas, tobacco, cotton
Major international organizations CIS, UN, UNESCO, WHO

Kyrgyzstan, part of the former Soviet Union, is a mountainous republic sharing a long southeastern border with China, and bounded to the north and west by three other Muslim republics of the CIS — Kazakhstan, Uzbekistan and Turkmenistan. The Kirghiz are renowned for their horsemanship, and use horses for rounding up and tending livestock, the main agricultural activity. In addition, Kyrgyzstan is self-sufficient in grain, and other crops including cotton and tobacco are grown widely for export. Industry (especially food processing, textiles and footwear) is well developed and benefits from the country's plentiful resources of fossil fuel.

LAOS

Land area 236,800 sq km (91,400 sq mi)
Major physical features highest point:
Phou Bia 2,820 m (9,251 ft); longest river:
Mekong (part) 4,180 km (2,600 mi)
Population (1994) 4,701,654
Form of government one-party (Communist)
republic with one legislative house
Capital city Vientiane (377,000)
Official language Lao
Ethnic composition Lao 67.1%; Palaung-Wa
11.9%; Tai 7.9%; Miao/Yao 5.2%; Mon-Khmer
4.6%; others 3.3%
Religious affiliations Buddhist 57.8%;

traditional beliefs 33.6%; nonreligious 4.8%;
Christian 1.8%; Muslim 1.0%; others 1.0%
Currency 1 new kip (NK) = 100 at
Economy Gross national product (per capita
1993) US $280; Gross domestic product
(1993) UN $1,334 million
Life expectancy at birth male 50.2 yr;
female 53.3 yr
Major resources coffee, tobacco, timber,
cotton, tin, gold, gemstones
Major international organizations IBRD,
IMF, NAM, UN, UNESCO, WHO

Laos is the only landlocked state in Southeast Asia. Mountainous and heavily forested,
its population is one of the lowest in the region. It was a French protectorate from 1893
to 1953, but independence was followed by civil unrest between Communist and
Monarchist forces, and involvement in the Vietnam War escalated the conflict. A new
constitution in 1991 provided for a president to be elected five-yearly. Cash crops (coffee, tobacco, cotton) are the mainstay of the economy, along with illegal opium exports.

LATVIA

Land area 64,500 sq km (24,900 sq mi)

Major physical features highest point: Vidzeme 311 m (1,020 ft); longest river: Western Dvina = Daugava (part) 1,060 km (635 mi)

Population (1994) 2,749,211

Form of government multiparty republic with one legislative house

Largest cities Riga (capital – 917,000); Daugavpils (128,000); Liepāja (115,000)

Official language Lettish

Ethnic composition Latvian 51.8%; Russian 33.8%; Belorussian 4.5%; Ukrainian 3.5%; Polish 2.3%; Lithuanian 1.3%; others 2.8%

Religious affiliations Lutheran, with Eastern Orthodox and Roman Catholic minorities

Currency 1 lat = 100 cents (November 1993)

Economy Gross national product (per capita 1993) US $2,010; Gross domestic product (1993) US $4,601 million

Life expectancy at birth male 64.4 yr; female 74.8 yr

Major resources amber, timber, peat, dairy produce, limestone

Major international organizations IBRD, IMF, UN, UNESCO, WHO

Latvia, on the eastern shores of the Baltic Sea, is one of the smallest of the republics that made up the former Soviet Union. The landscape consists of undulating plains, rising in the east to a low plateau dotted with lakes and bogs. Under the Soviet regime Latvia was heavily industrialized (industry accounted for 60 percent of GNP), but since independence traditional forestry, dairy farming and fishing are being reintroduced. The capital, Riga, is a busy port and trading center.

LEBANON

Land area   10,230 sq km (3,950 sq mi)
Major physical features   highest point: Qurnet es Sauda 3,087 m (10,128 ft); longest river: Litani 145 km (90 mi)
Population   (1994) 3,620,395
Form of government   multiparty republic with one legislative house
Largest cities   Beirut (capital – 1,500,000); Tripoli (500,000)
Official language   Arabic; French
Ethnic composition   Lebanese 82.6%; Palestinian 9.6%; Armenian 4.9%; others 2.9%
Religious affiliations   Shi'ite Muslim 32.0%; Maronite Christian 24.5%; Sunni Muslim 21.0%; Druze 7.0%; Greek Orthodox 6.5%; Greek Catholic 4.0%; Armenian Christian 4.0%; others 1.0%
Currency   1 Lebanese pound = 100 piastres
Economy   Gross national product (per capita 1991) US $2,000
Life expectancy at birth   male 66.9 yr; female 71.9 yr
Major resources   apples, grapes, citrus fruit, limestone, iron ore, precious metals, water
Major international organizations   IBRD, IMF, UN, UNESCO, UNHCR, WHO

Lebanon is a small mountainous country on the eastern Mediterranean coast, between Israel and Syria. The climate is milder and wetter than in most parts of the Middle East, and Lebanon has abundant water in a dry region. A bitter civil war 1975–90 did immeasurable damage to the economy, so that despite rich agricultural land and mineral resources, a strong banking sector, and successful manufacturing industry, Lebanon is currently in need of emergency aid. New foreign investment is desperately needed.

LESOTHO

Land area 30,355 sq km (11,720 sq mi)
Major physical feature highest point:
Thabana-Ntlenyana 3,482 m (11,425 ft)
Population (1994) 1,944,493
Form of government monarchy with
military government
Capital city Maseru (109,000)
Official languages Sesotho, English
Ethnic composition Sotho 99.7%; others 0.3%
Official religion Christianity
Religious affiliations Roman Catholic
43.5%; Protestant 41.3%; other Christians

8.0%; traditional beliefs 6.2%; others 1.0%
Currency 1 loti (plural maloti) = 100 lisente
Economy Gross national product (per capita
1993) US $650; Gross domestic product
(1993) US $609 million
Life expectancy at birth male 60.3 yr;
female 64.0 yr
Major resources water, agricultural and
grazing land, diamonds, wool, mohair, hides
Major international organizations GATT,
IBRD, IMF, NAM, UN, UNESCO, UNHCR, WHO

Lesotho is a small kingdom near the southern tip of Africa, completely surrounded by its powerful neighbor, South Africa. The landscape is low-lying with relatively high rainfall; in fact, in the absence of mineral deposits, water is one of Lesotho's few valuable resources. Economically the country is almost completely dependent on South Africa. A high proportion of Lesothan workers are employed in South African mines and their remittances form a large part of the country's revenue. Diamond mining is completely controlled by De Beers consolidated mines of South Africa. Agriculture is very limited, yields are low, and malnutrition is widespread.

LIBERIA

Land area 99,067 sq km (38,250 sq mi)
Major physical features highest point: Mount Wutivi 1,380 m (4,528 ft); longest river: Cavally (part) 515 km (320 mi)
Population (1994) 2,972,766
Form of government multiparty republic with two legislative houses
Capital city Monrovia (425,000)
Official language English
Ethnic composition African tribes (Kpelle, Bazza, Gio, Kru, Grebo, Mano, Krahn, Gola, Gbandi, Loma, Kissi, Vai and Bella) 95.0%; Americo-Liberian (descendants of slaves) 5%

Religious affiliations traditional beliefs 70.0%; Muslim 20.0%; Christian 10.0%
Currency 1 Liberian dollar (L$) = 100 cents
Economy Gross national product (per capita 1991) US $600
Life expectancy at birth male 55.3 yr; female 60.2 yr
Major resources iron ore, rubber, timber, coffee, diamonds, gold, water, fisheries, hydropower
Major international organizations IBRD, IMF, NAM, UN, UNESCO, WHO

Liberia, on the western Atlantic coast of Africa, is the continent's oldest republic. In 1822 a group of liberated slaves from America repatriated themselves to found a colony in the region, and in 1847 Liberia was internationally recognized as a nation. The economy relied on rubber exports; the Firestone Tire and Rubber Company of the United States made massive investments in the 1920s and Liberian rubber was essential to the Allied victory in World War II. Today iron ore has overtaken rubber as the chief export, and timber from the central rainforests is also an important source of revenue.

LIBYA

Land area 1,757,000 sq km (678,400 sq mi)
Major physical feature highest point: Bette 2,286 m (7,500 ft)
Population (1994) 5,057,392
Form of government Jamahiriya a "state of the masses" in practice a military dictatorship
Largest cities Tripoli (capital – 980,000); Benghazi (650,000); Misurata (117,000); Derna (105,000)
Official language Arabic
Ethnic composition Arab/Berber 97.0%; others 3.0%

Official religion Islam
Religious affiliations Sunni Muslim 97.0%; others 3.0%
Currency 1 Libyan dinar = 1,000 dirhams
Economy Gross national product (per capita 1991) US $5,500
Life expectancy at birth male 61.73 yr; female 66.1 yr
Major resources petroleum, natural gas, gypsum, potash, lignite, iron ore
Major international organizations IBRD, IMF, OAPEC, OPEC, UN, UNESCO, WHO

Libya is one of the world's wealthiest countries, with a remarkably high standard of living. Its wealth and enormous energy resources are derived from its oil reserves, exploited under government control. The head of state, Colonel Muammar Qaddafi, overthrew the monarchy in a military coup in 1969, and retains control as the "Revolutionary Leader" with the help of the armed forces and a few close advisers. Qaddafi openly supports terrorist organizations in the interests of Arab nationalism.

LIECHTENSTEIN

Land area 160 sq km (62 sq mi)
Major physical feature highest point: Grauspitz 2,623 m (8,606 ft)
Population (1994) 30,281
Form of government multiparty constitutional monarchy with one legislative house
Capital city Vaduz (5,000)
Official language German
Ethnic composition Liechtensteiner 63.6%; Swiss 15.7%; Austrian 7.7%; German 3.7%; others 9.3%

Religious affiliations Roman Catholic 87.3%; Protestant 8.3%; others 4.4%
Currency 1 Swiss franc = 100 centimes
Economy Gross national product (per capita 1991) US $33,000
Life expectancy at birth male 73.8 yr; female 81.0 yr
Major resources financial services, tourism, postage stamps
Major international organizations EFTA, IAEA, UN

Liechtenstein is a tiny principality on the east bank of the upper Rhine, between Austria and Switzerland. To the north and west the land is a broad floodplain bordering the Rhine; to the east the foothills of the Alps rise to snow-capped peaks along the southern border. About two fifths of the land area is forested, with Alpine plants growing above the treeline. Although Liechtenstein uses Swiss currency and belongs to the Swiss customs union, it is a fully independent state. The economy depends on revenue earned through the banking sector; advantageous tax and company legislation have made the principality a thriving business center with thousands of companies registered there. Tourism is also a major earner of revenue, and the sale of decorative postage stamps to international collectors accounts for about 10 percent of national income.

LITHUANIA

Land area 65,200 sq km (25,200 sq mi)
Major physical features highest point:
Juozapine 294 m (964 ft); longest river:
Neman (part) 970 km (580 mi)
Population (1994) 3,848,389
Form of government multiparty republic
with one legislative house
Largest cities Vilnius (capital – 593,000);
Kaunas (430,000); Klaipeda (206,000)
Official language Lithuanian
Ethnic composition Lithuanian 80.1%;
Russian 8.6%; Polish 7.7%; Belorussian 1.5%;
others 2.1%

Religious affiliations mainly Roman
Catholic, with Lutheran and Reformed
minorities
Currency litas (since June 1993)
Economy Gross national product (per capita
1993) US $1,320; Gross domestic product
(1993) US $4,335 million
Life expectancy at birth male 66.5 yr;
female 76.2 yr
Major resources beef and dairy products,
timber, peat, petroleum, limestone
Major international organizations IBRD,
IMF, UN, UNESCO

Lithuania lies on the southeastern corner of the Baltic Sea. The terrain is low-lying with
sand dunes along the coast and lake-strewn hills in the southeast. The country came
under Russian domination in the 18th century and did not regain independence until
the breakup of the Soviet Union in 1991, but the local culture was kept alive during the
Soviet era through folk art. Under the Soviets, Lithuania received fewer immigrants than
Latvia and Estonia, and managed to maintain its Roman Catholic tradition. The state is
undergoing a difficult change from a command to a free-market economy.

LUXEMBOURG

Land area   2,586 sq km (999 sq mi)
Major physical features   highest point: Wemperhardt 559 m (1,843 ft); longest river: Moselle (part) 240 km (150 mi)
Population   (1994) 401,900
Form of government   multiparty constitutional monarchy with one legislative house
Capital city   Luxembourg (76,000)
Official languages   French, German, Letzeburgesch
Ethnic composition   Luxembourger 72.5%; Portuguese 9.0%; Italian 5.4%; French 3.4%; Belgian 2.5%; German 2.4%; others 4.8%
Religious affiliations   Roman Catholic 93.0%; Protestant 1.3%; others 5.7%
Currency   1 Luxembourg franc = 100 centimes
Economy   Gross national product (per capita 1991) US $31,080
Life expectancy at birth   male 73.0 yr; female 80.5 yr
Major resources   banking services, tourism
Major international organizations   EU, GATT, IBRD, IMF, NATO, UN, UNESCO, UNPROFOR, WHO

Luxembourg is a tiny landlocked state wedged between Belgium, Germany and France. It is a constitutional monarchy, with a democratically elected government headed by the Grand Duke. In spite of the strong influence of its larger neighbors, Luxembourg retains a strong sense of cultural identity, and has preserved its own language, Letzeburgesch, alongside French and German. Two thirds of the terrain (the central and southern region) is in the basins of the rivers Sûre and Alzette, where beds of iron ore are covered by fertile soil and thick woodland. The north of the country is a high plateau, forested in parts, but mostly arid and barren. The economy depends almost entirely on financial services and manufacturing from imported raw materials. Favorable tax laws draw companies to register there, and Luxembourg boasts over 160 banks.

MACEDONIA,
Former Yugoslav Republic of

Land area 25,713 sq km (9,928 sq mi)

Major physical features highest point: Korab Mountains (east) 2,764 m (9,066 ft); longest river: Vardar 388 km (241 mi)

Population (1994) 2,213,785

Form of government emerging democracy

Capital city Skopje (563,000)

Official language Macedonian

Ethnic composition Macedonian 65.0%; Albanian 22.0%; Turkish 4.0%; Serb 2.0%; gypsies 3.0%; others 4.0%

Religious affiliations Eastern Orthodox 67.0%; Muslim 30.0%; others 3.0%

Currency 1 dinar =100 paras (since April 1992)

Economy Gross national product (per capita 1993) US $820; Gross domestic product (1993) US $1,704 million

Life expectancy at birth male 71.5 yr; female 75.8 yr

Major resources chromium, lead, zinc, manganese, tungsten, nickel, iron ore, timber

Major international organizations IMF, UN, UNESCO, WHO

The Former Yugoslav Republic of Macedonia came into being in September 1991 on the breakup of Yugoslavia. It is the least prosperous of the new republics in the region.

MADAGASCAR

Land area 587,041 sq km (226,658 sq mi)
Major physical features highest point: Tsaratanana Massif 2,876 m (9,436 ft); longest river: Mangoky 560 km (350 mi)
Population (1994) 13,427,758
Form of government multiparty republic with one legislative house
Capital city Antananarivo (802,000)
Official languages Malagasy, French
Ethnic composition Malagasy 98.9%; Comorian 0.3%; Indian 0.2%; French 0.2%; others 0.4%
Religious affiliations traditional beliefs 47.0%; Roman Catholic 26.0%; Protestant 22.8%; other Christians 2.2%; Muslim 1.7%; others 0.3%
Currency 1 Malagasy franc = 100 centimes
Economy Gross national product (per capita 1993) US $220; Gross domestic product (1993) US $3,126 million
Life expectancy at birth male 52.0 yr; female 56.0 yr
Major resources coffee, vanilla, graphite, chromite, coal, gold, semiprecious stones
Major international organizations GATT, IBRD, IMF, NAM, UN, UNESCO, UNHCR, WHO

Madagascar, the fourth largest island in the world, lies off the southeast coast of Africa, opposite Mozambique. Its unique and diverse flora and wildlife are quite distinct from those on the mainland, but many rare species are severely endangered. The economy depends on traditional cash crops and small-scale mining of minerals.

MALAWI

Land area 94,276 sq km (36,400 sq mi)
Major physical features highest point: Mount Mulanje 3,000 m (9,843 ft); longest river: Shire (part) 400 km (250 mi); largest lake: Lake Malawi 29,600 sq km (11,400 sq mi)
Population (1994) 9,732,409
Form of government one-party republic with one legislative house
Largest cities Blantyre (332,000); Lilongwe (capital – 234,000); Mzuzu (83,000)
Official language English
Ethnic composition Maravi 58.3%; Lomwe 18.4%; Yao 13.2%; Ngoni 6.7%; others 3.4%

Religious affiliations Protestant 55.0%; Catholic 20.0%; Muslim 20.0%; others 5.0%
Currency 1 Malawian kwacha = 100 tambala
Economy Gross national product (per capita 1993) US $200; Gross domestic product (1993) US $1,810 million
Life expectancy at birth male 38.9 yr; female 40.5 yr
Major resources tobacco, tea, sugar, coffee, peanuts, wood products, limestone, unexploited uranium, coal and bauxite
Major international organizations GATT, IBRD, IMF, NAM, UN, UNESCO, WHO

Malawi is a land locked state at the southern end of the East African Rift Valley, sharing borders with Zambia, Tanzania and Mozambique. The economy is predominantly agricultural, and export earnings are vulnerable to fluctuating prices and bad weather. Following a severe drought in 1992 Malawi is dependent on aid from the IMF, the World Bank and individual donations from other states.

MALAYSIA

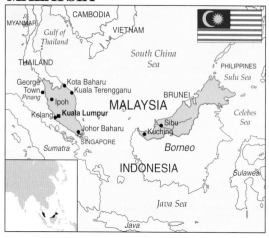

Land area 330,442 sq km (127,584 sq mi)

Major physical features highest point: Mount Kinabalu 4,094 m (13,452 ft); longest river: Rajang (Borneo) 560 km (350 mi)

Population (1994) 19,283,157

Form of government multiparty constitutional monarchy with two legislative houses

Largest cities Kuala Lumpur (capital – 938,000); Ipoh (301,000); George Town (Pinang, 251,000)

Official language Bahasa Malaysian

Ethnic composition Malay and other indigenous peoples 61.4%; Chinese 30.0%; Indian 8.1%; others 0.5%

Official religion Islam

Religious affiliations Muslim 52.9%; Buddhist 17.3%; Chinese folk religions 11.6%; Hindu 7.0%; Christian 6.4%; others 4.8%

Currency 1 ringgit (M$) = 100 sen

Economy Gross national product (per capita 1993) US $3,140; Gross domestic product (1993) US $64,450 million

Life expectancy at birth male 66.3 yr; female 72.9 yr

Major resources rubber, palm oil, tin, petroleum, timber, copper, iron ore, natural gas

Major international organizations GATT, IBRD, IMF, NAM, UN, UNESCO, WHO

Malaysia is made up of west Malaysia on the southern tip of the Southeast Asian mainland, and the states of Sabah and Sarawak on the island of Borneo. The territory has a long history of invasion, creating a rich ethnic mix (and some conflict) and the component parts of the nation have been split up and recombined in dozens of formations. Today it is a constitutional monarchy made up of 13 states, rich in cash crops and valuable mineral resources, and with one of the strongest economies in the region.

MALDIVES

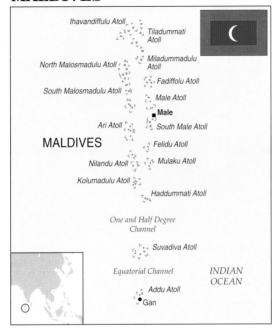

Land area 288 sq km (115 sq mi)
Population (1994) 252,077
Form of government nonparty republic with one legislative house
Capital city Male (55,000)
Official language Divehi
Ethnic composition Sinhalese, Dravidian, Arab, African (figures not available)
Official religion Islam

Religious affiliations Sunni Muslim 100.0%
Currency 1 Maldivian rufiyaa = 100 laari
Economy Gross national product (per capita 1991) US $460
Life expectancy at birth male 63.2 yr; female 66.2 yr
Major resources fish
Major international organizations ESCAP, GATT, IBRD, IMF, NAM, UN, UNESCO, WHO

Maldives is a chain of some 19 island groups (almost 2,000 islands, some of them atolls) in the Indian Ocean off the southwest coast of India and Sri Lanka. Fishing and subsistence agriculture are the main activities and tourism is on the increase.

MALI

Land area 1,240,192 sq km (478,841 sq mi)
Major physical features highest point: Hombori Tondo 1,155 m (3,789 ft); longest river: Niger (part) 4,200 km (2,600 mi)
Population (1994) 9,112,950
Form of government one-party republic with one legislative house
Capital city Bamako (646,000)
Official language French
Ethnic composition Bambara 31.9%; Fulani 13.9%; Senufo 12.0%; Soninke 8.8%; Tuareg 7.3%; Songhai 7.2%; Malinke 6.6%; Dogon 4.0%; Dyula 2.9%; Bobo 2.4%; Arab 1.2%; others 1.8%

Religious affiliations Sunni Muslim 90.0%; traditional beliefs 9.0%; Christian 1.0%
Currency 1 CFA franc = 100 centimes
Economy Gross national product (per capita 1993) US $270; Gross domestic product (1993) US $2,662 million
Life expectancy at birth male 44.0 yr; female 47.0 yr
Major resources gold, phosphates, kaolin, salt, limestone, uranium, bauxite, iron ore
Major international organizations GATT, IBRD, IMF, NAM, UN, UNESCO, WHO

The landlocked state of Mali lies in the Sahal area of northwest Africa on the fringes of the Sahara. About 70% of the land area is desert or semidesert, but the vast majority of the population makes their living from agriculture and fishing in the Niger valley.

MALTA

Land area 316 sq km (122 sq mi)
Major physical features largest island: Malta 246 sq km (95 sq mi); highest point: southwest cliffs 253 m (830 ft)
Population (1994) 366,767
Form of government multiparty republic with one legislative house
Capital city Valletta (102,000)
Official languages Maltese, English
Ethnic composition Maltese 95.7%; British 2.1%; others 2.2%
Official religion Roman Catholicism

Religious affiliations Roman Catholic 97.3%; Anglican 1.2%; others 1.5%
Currency 1 Maltese lira (Lm) = 100 cents = 1,000 mils
Economy Gross national product (per capita 1991) US $6,850
Life expectancy at birth male 74.5 yr; female 79.2 yr
Major resources port facilities, tourism, limestone, salt
Major international organizations GATT, IMF, NAM, UN, UNESCO, WHO

The republic of Malta consists of the islands of Malta, Gozo and Comino in narrow straits of the Mediterranean between Sicily and Tunisia in north Africa. The position is a strategically important one and the republic has changed hands several times in its history. The islands are the peaks of a massive limestone outcrop stretching south from Sicily. Natural vegetation is sparse due to erosion and overgrazing, and there are no freshwater supplies (apart from rainfall). Desalinization plants are used extensively to provide a stable water supply. The economy depends largely on shipping and port facilities, but there is small-scale manufacturing in the electronics and garment industries. Tourism is the largest single source of foreign exchange.

MARSHALL ISLANDS

Land area 181 sq km (70 sq mi)

Population (1994) 54, 031

Form of government Democratic republic with two legislative houses

Capital city Dalap-Uliga-Darrit

Official language English

Ethnic composition Marshallese (a micronesian people) 97%; others 3%

Religious affiliations Christian (Protestant)

Currency 1 United States dollar = 100 cents

Economy Gross national product (per capita 1994) US $1,313

Life expectancy at birth male 61.6 yr; female 64.7 yr

Major resources phosphates, iron ore, fisheries, deep seabed minerals, copper, gold

Major international organizations ESCAP, IBRD, IMF, UN, WHO

The Marshall Islands are a group of 5 single islands, 31 widely separated coral atolls (including the largest atoll in the world) and over 1,000 islets and reefs strung out in two chains in the western Pacific Ocean. From 1949 until 1979 they were part of the Trust Territory of the United States, then they became self-governing in free association with the US, and in 1992 they became politically autonomous. Local politics are traditionally dominated by the island chiefs, and their high chief holds the post of president, but the economy of the Marshall Islands is still heavily dependent on aid from the US, and the rent paid by its benefactor for the use of Kwajalein atoll as a US missile base. The tourist industry is an important source of foreign revenue and employment, but all other industry is small-scale and limited to handicrafts, and processing fish or copra. Agriculture is mainly at subsistence level, but some cash crops — coconuts, tomatoes, melons and breadfruit — are grown in small quantities on local farms.

MAURITANIA

Land area 1,030,700 sq km (389,000 sq mi)

Major physical feature highest point: Kediat Idjil 915 m (3,002 ft)

Population (1994) 2,192,777

Form of government republic with military government

Capital city Nouakchott (393,000)

Official languages Pulaar; Soninke; Wolof

Ethnic composition Moorish 81.5%; Wolof 6.8%; Tukulor 5.3%; Soninke 2.8%; Fulani 1.1%; others 2.5%

Official religion Islam

Religious affiliations Sunni Muslim 99.4%; Christian 0.4%; others 0.2%

Currency 1 ouguiya (UM) = 5 khoums

Economy Gross national product (per capita 1993) US $500; Gross domestic product (1993) US $859 million

Life expectancy at birth male 45.2 yr; female 51.0 yr

Major resources iron ore, gypsum, fish, copper, phosphate, gum arabic

Major international organizations GATT, IBRD, IMF, NAM, UN, UNESCO, WHO

Mauritania extends from the Atlantic coast of West Africa northward to the Sahara. The coastal plains and valley of the Senegal river are fertile areas where farming is concentrated; north and east are tableland plateaus and the sand dunes of the Sahara. Fishing and mining the country's deposits of iron and copper are the main economic activities.

MAURITIUS

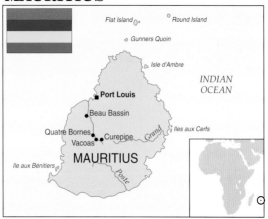

Land area 2,040 sq km (788 sq mi)
Major physical features highest point: Piton de la Petite Rivière Noire 826 m (2,711 ft); largest island: Mauritius 1,865 sq km (720 sq mi)
Population (1994) 1,116,923
Form of government multiparty republic with one legislative house
Capital city Port Louis (143,000)
Official language English
Ethnic composition Indo-mauritian 68.0%; Creole 27.0%; Sino-mauritian 3.0%; Franco-mauritian 2.0%

Religious affiliations Hindu 52.5%; Roman Catholic 25.7%; Muslim 12.9%; Protestant 4.4%; Buddhist 0.4%; others 4.1%
Currency 1 rupee = 100 cents
Economy Gross national product (per capita 1993) US $3,030; Gross domestic product (1993) US $2,780 million
Life expectancy at birth male 66.6 yr; female 74.6 yr
Major resources iron ore, gypsum, fish, copper, phosphate
Major international organizations GATT, IBRD, IMF, NAM, UN, UNESCO, WHO

Mauritius, one of the Mascarene Islands, is an island state in the Indian Ocean some 800 km (500 mi) east of Madagascar. Its territory includes the volcanic island Rodrigues, and the tiny dependency of the Agalegals to the north. The main island is a volcanic outcrop fringed with coral reefs, with a broad coastal plain rising to the remains of a giant volcano. The French colonized the islands in the 18th century, and imported African slaves to work their sugar plantations. The territory was ceded to Britain in 1810 and gained independence within the Commonwealth in 1968. Mauritius remains dependent on sugar cane, despite efforts to diversify into tea, bananas, tobacco and fisheries.

MEXICO

Land area 1,958,201 sq km (756,066 sq mi)
Major physical features highest point: Citlaltépetl 5,699 m (18,700 ft); longest river: Rio Grande (part) 2,100 km (1,300 mi)
Population (1994) 92,202,199
Form of government federal multiparty republic with two legislative houses
Largest cities Mexico City (capital – 13,636,000); Guadalajara (2,847,000); Monterrey (2,522,000); Puebla (1,055,000)
Official language Spanish
Ethnic composition mestizo 55%; Amerindian 29%; white 15%; black 0.5%; others 0.5%

Religious affiliations Roman Catholic 92.6%; Protestant 3.3%; nonreligious 3.1%; Jewish 0.1%; others 0.9%
Currency 1 New Mexican peso = 100 centavos
Economy Gross national product (per capita 1993) US $3,610; Gross domestic product (1993) US $343,472 million
Life expectancy at birth male 69.4 yr; female 76.7 yr
Major resources petroleum, silver, copper, gold, lead, zinc, natural gas, timber
Major international organizations CARICOM, GATT, IBRD, IMF, LAES, UN, WHO

Mexico is the largest of the Latin-American states, occupying the mountainous and geologically unstable bridge of land linking North and South America, and stretching between the Pacific Ocean and the Gulf of Mexico. The country is rich in natural resources; it has the world's largest deposits of silver, large deposits of copper, zinc, and lead, and recently it has begun to develop manufacturing industry, drawing on massive resources of oil, natural gas and hydropower, and an inexpensive labor force. However, rapid economic growth is offset by the soaring population, falling oil prices, the long-term repercussions of the 1985 Mexico City earthquake, and massive foreign debt.

MOLDOVA

Land area 33,700 sq km (13,000 sq mi)
Major physical features highest point: Balaneshty 430 m (1,409 ft); longest river: Dniester (part) 1,420 km (880 mi)
Population (1994) 4,473,033
Form of government multiparty republic with one legislative house
Largest cities Chisinau (capital – 676,000); Tiraspol (184,000); Beltsy (162,000)
Official language Moldovan (Romanian)
Ethnic composition Moldovan 64.5%; Ukrainian 13.8%; Russian 13.0%; Gagauz 3.5%; Jewish 1.5%; Bulgarian 2.0%; others 1.7%

Religious affiliations Eastern Orthodox 98.5%; Jewish 1.5%
Currency the len (since late 1993)
Economy Gross national product (per capita 1993) US $1,060; Gross domestic product (1993) US $4,292 million
Life expectancy at birth male 64.7 yr; female 71.7 yr
Major resources grapes (for wine), tobacco, fruit and vegetables, lignite, phosphates
Major international organizations CIS, IBRD, IMF, UN, UNESCO, WHO

Moldova became an independent republic in 1991 with the breakup of the Soviet Union. Since then it has introduced bold economic reforms, establishing its own currency and privatizing industry. The economy is based on agriculture; mineral resources are sparse.

MONACO

Land area 1.95 sq km (0.75 sq mi)
Major physical features none
Population (1994) 30,000
Form of government nonparty constitutional monarchy with two legislative houses
Capital city Monaco (30,000)
Official language French
Ethnic composition French 47%; Monégasque 16%; Italian 16%; others 21%

Official religion Roman Catholicism
Religious affiliations Roman Catholic 95.0%; others 5.0%
Currency 1 French franc = 100 centimes
Life expectancy at birth male 73.9 yr; female 81.6 yr
Major resources tourism, financial services
Major international organizations UN, UNESCO, WHO

The tiny principality of Monaco lies on the Mediterranean coast just to the east of Nice and very close to the Italian border. Monte Carlo is a fashionable resort, famous for its casinos and for glittering productions of opera and ballet. The principality is also host to two international motor sport events, the Monte Carlo rally and the Monaco Grand Prix. The Grimaldi family has ruled Monaco since 1297, with a break in 1793 when the state declared itself a republic in 1792 and came under the control of revolutionary France in 1793. The Grimaldis were restored to power in 1861, and a treaty with France since 1918 guarantees Monaco's autonomy even if the Grimaldi family dies out. The economy depends on financial services, and has set itself up as a tax haven for wealthy individuals. There is no income tax, and business taxes are very low for any companies registered in the principality. There are also a small number of high-value non-polluting industries, and a thriving tourist industry.

MONGOLIA

Land area 1,566,500 sq km (604,800 sq mi)

Major physical features highest point: Hüyten (Nayramdal) Peak 4,374 m (14,350 ft); longest river: Selenga 1,000 km (620 mi)

Population (1994) 2,429,762

Form of government multiparty republic with two legislative houses

Capital city Ulan Bator (575,000)

Official language Khalkha Mongolian

Ethnic composition Khalkha Mongol 77.5%; Kazakh 5.3%; Dörbed Mongol 2.8%; Bayad 2.0%; Buryat Mongol 1.9%; Dariganga Mongol 1.5%; others 9.0%

Religious affiliations Shamanist, Buddhist, Muslim (figures not available)

Currency 1 tugrik (Tug) = 100 möngös

Economy Gross national product (per capita 1993) US $390; Gross domestic product (1993) US $539 million

Life expectancy at birth male 63.9 yr; female 68.5 yr

Major resources oil, coal, copper, tungsten, molybdenum, phosphates, tin, nickle, zinc, gold, fluorspar

Major international organizations IBRD, IMF, NAM, UN, UNESCO, WHO

Mongolia is a large landlocked republic with China on its southern frontier and Russia to the north. It is often known as Outer Mongolia to distinguish it from Inner Mongolia, an autonomous region of China. Most of the country is over 1,000 m (3,300 ft) above sea level, with the highest peaks in the Altai mountains of the central Hangayan range. Almost four fifths of the terrain is dry steppe grassland, which supports livestock (sheep, goats, horses, and cattle). Much of the rest is cold, arid desert. Large deposits of fossil fuels and minerals support the economy, and industry processes raw materials.

MOROCCO

Land area 458,730 sq km (177,117 sq mi)

Major physical features highest point: Toubkal 4,165 m (13,665 ft); longest river: Moulouya 515 km (320 mi)

Population (1994) 28,558,635

Form of government multiparty constitutional monarchy with one legislative house

Largest cities Casablanca (2,409,000); Rabat (capital – 893,000); Marrakesh (549,000)

Official language Arabic

Ethnic composition Arab/Berber 99.1%; Jewish 0.2%; others 0.7%

Official religion Islam

Religious affiliations Sunni Muslim 98.7%; Christian 1.1%; others 0.2%

Currency 1 Moroccan dirham = 100 centimes

Economy Gross national product (per capita 1993) US $1,040; Gross domestic product (1993) US $26,635 million

Life expectancy at birth male 66.4 yr; female 70.2 yr

Major resources phosphates, iron ore, lead, manganese, zinc, fisheries, salt, tourism

Major international organizations GATT, IBRD, IMF, NAM, UNESCO, UNHCR, WHO

Morocco, in northwestern Africa, is one of the few remaining monarchies in the Arab world. The adjoining territory of Western Sahara is under Moroccan control, though its status is disputed. The Atlas Mountains run through the center of the country, spreading into high plateaus along the Algerian border. The northwestern coastal plains are fertile areas where the population is concentrated. Despite rich natural resources, Morocco suffers from debt and high unemployment; recurring drought hampers economic growth.

MOZAMBIQUE

Land area 799,379 sq km (308,642 sq mi)
Major physical feature highest point:
Monte Binga 2,436 m (7,992 ft)
Population (1994) 17,346,000
Form of government one-party republic
with one legislative house
Largest cities Maputo (capital – 1,070,000);
Beira (270,000); Nampula (183,000)
Official language Portuguese
Ethnic composition Makua 47.3%; Tsonga
23.3%; Malawi 12.0%; Shona 11.3%; Yao 3.8%;
Swahili 0.8%; Makonde 0.6%; Portuguese 0.2%;

others 0.7%
Religious affiliations traditional beliefs
47.8%; Roman Catholic 31.4%; Muslim 13.0%;
Protestant 7.5%; others 0.3%
Currency 1 metical (Mt) = 100 centavos
Economy Gross national product (per capita
1993) US $90; Gross domestic product (1993)
US $1,367 million
Major resources cashew nuts, cotton, sugar
cane, copra, citrus fruits, fish, coal, titanium
Major international organizations GATT,
IBRD, IMF, NAM, UN, UNESCO, WHO

Mozambique is on Africa's southeastern coast, facing Madagascar. The coastal plain
occupies most of the south, but further inland the landscape rises in steps to the table-
lands of the High Veld. Until recently, South Africa's policy of destabilization has prevented Mozambique from exploiting its excellent agricultural resources and hydropower.

MYANMAR

Land area 676,577 sq km (261,228 sq mi)
Major physical features highest point: Hkakabo Razi 5,881 m (19,296 ft); longest river: Irrawaddy 1,092 km (1,300 mi)
Population (1994) 44,277,014
Form of government military regime
Largest cities Rangoon (capital – 2,513,000); Mandalay (533,000)
Official language Burmese
Ethnic composition Burman 68.0%; Shan 9.0%; Karen 7.0%; Rakhine 4.0%; Chinese 3.0%; Mon 2.0%; Indian 2.0%; others 5.0%

Religious affiliations Buddhist 89.0%; Christian 4.0%; Muslim 4.0%; animist beliefs 1.0%; others 2.0%
Currency 1 kyat (K) = 100 pyas
Economy Gross national product (per capita 1991) US $500
Life expectancy at birth male 57.9 yr; female 62.1 yr
Major resources rice, pulses, timber, opium, tin, petroleum, precious stones, natural gas
Major international organizations GATT, IBRD, IMF, NAM, UN, UNESCO, WHO

Myanmar, formerly Burma, is the westernmost of the Southeast Asian countries. For centuries its chief export has been rice, though timber and opium are also important.

NAMIBIA

Land area 823,144 sq km (317,818 sq mi)
Major physical feature highest point: Brandberg 2,606 m (8,550 ft)
Population (1994) 1,596,000
Form of government multiparty republic with two legislative houses
Capital city Windhoek (115,000)
Official languages English, Afrikaans
Ethnic composition Ovambo 49.8%; Kavango 9.3%; Herero 7.5%; Damara 7.5%; European 6.4%; Nama (Hottentots) 4.8%; others 14.7%

Religious affiliations Lutheran 51.2%; Roman Catholic 19.8%; Afrikaans Reformed 6.1%; Anglican 5.0%; others 17.9%
Currency 1 South African rand = 100 cents
Economy Gross national product (per capita 1993) US $1,820; Gross domestic product (1993) US $2,109 million
Major resources diamonds, copper, gold, uranium, lead, tin, natural gas, iron ore
Major international organizations GATT, IBRD, IMF, UN, UNESCO, UNHCR, WHO

Namibia, on the southwest coast of Africa, won independence from its powerful neighbor, South Africa, in 1990, but Namibia's main port, Walvis Bay was only ceded in May 1994. The majority of the population live by livestock farming and small-scale fishing. Namibia is dependent on South Africa for its food supply, and for manufactured goods. Although the country is rich in mineral resources, it exports most of them unprocessed.

NAURU

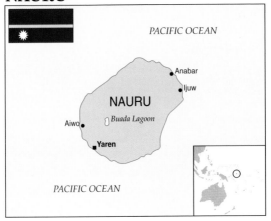

Land area   21 sq km (8 sq mi)
Major physical feature   highest point 69 m (225 ft)
Population   (1994) 10,000
Form of government   nonparty republic
Capital city   Yaren
Official languages   Nauruan, English
Ethnic composition   Nauruan 58.0%; other Pacific islanders 26.0%; Chinese 8.0%; European 8.0%
Religious affiliations   Protestant 58.0%; Roman Catholic 24.0%; others 18.0%
Currency   1 Australian dollar = 100 cents
Economy   Gross national product (per capita 1991) US $10,000
Life expectancy at birth   male 64.3 yr; female 69.2 yr
Major resources   phosphates

Nauru is a tiny single-island state in the western Pacific Ocean immediately south of the equator and about 700 km (450 mi) west of Kiribati. It is the world's smallest republic and has one of the highest per capita incomes in the world, thanks to a single natural resource — phosphate. The island is a raised coral reef with a central plateau where rich phosphate beds have been created by centuries of bird droppings. Japan, New Zealand, South Korea and Australia are all major customers for phosphate rock which they use as a fertilizer. In recent years heavy exploitation of the resource means that stocks will run out by the end of the 20th century, but sales have earned enough revenue for the government to support large-scale foreign investment providing income that should cushion the transition to a different economic structure. As mines fall into disuse the land is reclaimed for agriculture and Nauru is beginning to export cash crops of bananas, coconuts and pineapples.

NEPAL

Land area 147,181 sq km (56,827 sq mi)
Major physical features highest point: Mount Everest 8,848 m (29,028 ft); longest river: Ghaghara (part) 920 km (570 mi)
Population (1994) 21,041,000
Form of government multiparty constitutional monarchy with two legislative houses
Capital city Kathmandu (235,000)
Official language Nepali
Ethnic composition Nepalese 58.4%; Bihari 18.7%; Tharu 3.6%; Tamang 3.5%; Newar 3.0%; others 12.8%
Official religion Hinduism

Religious affiliations Hindu 89.5%; Buddhist 5.3%; Muslim 2.7%; Jain 0.1%; others 2.4%
Currency 1 Nepalese rupee = 100 paisa
Economy Gross national product (per capita 1993) US $190; Gross domestic product (1993) US $3,551 million
Life expectancy at birth male 52.3 yr; female 52.7 yr
Major resources quartz, water, timber, hydropower
Major international organizations IBRD, IMF, NAM, UN, UNESCO, UNPROFOR, WHO

Nepal is a small landlocked kingdom in southern Asia, lying between India and China. The Himalayas, including the world's highest peak, Mount Everest, stretch across the north of the country where alpine landscapes give way to permanent ice in the higher ranges, but in the lowlands of the south, traditionally regarded as the birthplace of the Buddha (563–438 BC), the climate is subtropical and sugar and jute are grown as cash crops. Industry is small-scale and limited to processing agricultural crops. However, tourism is expanding, especially in the Kathmandu region, where it is becoming an important source of foreign revenue.

NETHERLANDS

Land area 41,863 sq km (16,163 sq mi)

Major physical features highest point: Vaalserberg 321 m (1,053 ft); lowest point: -7 m (-22 ft); longest river: Rhine (part) 1,320 km (820 mi)

Population (1994) 15,368,000

Form of government multiparty constitutional monarchy with two legislative houses

Largest cities Amsterdam (capital – 1,091,000); Rotterdam (1,069,000); The Hague (693,000); Utrecht (543,000)

Official language Dutch

Ethnic composition Netherlands 95.8%; Turkish 1.2%; Moroccan 0.9%; German 0.3%; others 1.8%

Religious affiliations Roman Catholic 34.0%; Reformed 25.0%; nonreligious 36.0%; Muslim 3.0%; others 2.0%

Currency 1 Netherlands guilder = 100 cents

Economy Gross national product (per capita 1993) US $20,950; Gross domestic product (1993) US $309,227 million

Life expectancy at birth male 74.7 yr; female 81.0 yr

Major resources port facilities, natural gas, bulbs, cut flowers, dairy products, fruit, vegetables, petroleum

Major international organizations EU, GATT, IMF, UN, UNESCO, UNHCR, UNPROFOR, WHO

The Netherlands is a densely populated country on the northwest coast of Europe. Vast tracts of its land have been reclaimed from the sea. Benefiting from its key position at the mouth of the Rhine, it has become one of Europe's most prosperous states.

NEW ZEALAND

Land area 267,515 sq km (103,288 sq mi)
Major physical features highest point: Mount Cook 3,764 m (12,316 ft); largest lake: Lake Taupo 606 sq km (234 sq mi)
Population (1994) 3,389,000
Form of government multiparty constitutional monarchy with one legislative house
Largest cities Auckland (885,000); Wellington (capital – 325,000); Christchurch (307,000); Hamilton (148,000)
Official languages English, Maori
Ethnic composition European 88.0%; Maori 8.9%; other Polynesians 2.9%; others 0.2%

Religious affiliations Anglican 24.3%; Presbyterian 18%; nonreligious 16.4%; Roman Catholic 15.2%; Methodist 4.7%; others 21.4%
Currency 1 New Zealand dollar = 100 cents
Economy Gross national product (per capita 1993) US $12,600; Gross domestic product (1993) US $43,699 million
Life expectancy at birth male 72.7 yr; female 80.2 yr
Major resources natural gas, iron ore, sand, coal, timber, hydropower, gold, limestone
Major international organization GATT, IBRD, IMF, UN, UNESCO, UNPROFOR, WHO

New Zealand is an island state in the southwestern Pacific Ocean about 1,600 km (1,000 mi) southeast of Australia. It also encompasses the Cook Islands, Tokelau, and Niue.

NICARAGUA

Land area 120,349 sq km (46,467 sq mi)
Major physical feature highest point: Cerro
Mogotón 2,107 m (6,913 ft)
Population (1994) 4,097,000
Form of government multiparty republic
with one legislative house
Capital city Managua (682,000)
Official language Spanish
Ethnic composition mestizo 69.0%; white
17.0%; black 9.0%; Amerindian 5.0%
Religious affiliations Roman Catholic
95.0%; Protestant 5.0%

Currency 1 gold córdoba = 100 centavos
Economy Gross national product (per capita
1993) US $340; Gross domestic product
(1993) US $1,800 million
Life expectancy at birth male 61.2 yr;
female 66.9 yr
Major resources cotton, coffee, gold, silver,
copper, tungsten, lead, zinc, timber, fish
Major international organizations GATT,
IBRD, IMF, LAES, NAM, UN, UNESCO,
UNHCR, WHO

The Central American state of Nicaragua lies between Honduras to the northwest and
Costa Rica to the south. The eastern plains are bordered with lagoons and swamps, but
further inland the landscape rises toward the central highlands, and beyond them to
two ranges of volcanoes (some still active) and the massive Lake Nicaragua. Earthquakes and hurricanes are frequent hazards in the region. Civil war during the 1980s
caused long-term damage to the economy, but a stabilization program since 1991 has
reduced inflation and encouraged foreign investment. Cotton and coffee are the main
cash crops and gold and copper are intensively mined.

NIGER

Land area 1,186,408 sq km (458,075 sq mi)
Major physical features highest point: Mont Greboun 1,944 m (6,379 ft); longest river: Niger (part) 4,200 km (2,600 mi)
Population (1994) 8,972,000
Form of government one-party republic with one legislative house
Largest cities Niamey (capital – 398,000); Zinder (121,000); Maradi (113,000)
Official language French
Ethnic composition Hausa 54.1%; Songhai/Zerma/Dendi 21.7%; Fulani 10.1%; Tuareg 8.4%; Kanuri 4.2%; Teda 0.2%; others 1.3%

Religious affiliations Sunni Muslim 80.0%; traditional beliefs and Christian 20.0%
Currency 1 CFA franc = 100 centimes
Economy Gross national product (per capita 1993) US $270; Gross domestic product (1993) US $2,220 million
Life expectancy at birth male 43.0 yr; female 46.3 yr
Major resources uranium, ground nuts (peanuts) cotton, cattle and beef products, coal, iron ore, tin, phosphates
Major international organizations GATT, IBRD, IMF, NAM, UN, UNESCO, WHO

The republic of Niger is a landlocked country at the heart of northwestern Africa. It borders on seven other nations, and with them forms the Sahal region, notorious for its repeated droughts since the 1960s. Two thirds of Niger forms part of the Sahara; only the southwest, around the Niger river valley, has rich arable land, and the fringes of Lake Chad support savanna grassland. Until recent periods of drought, Niger was self-sufficient in food, and there are signs of recovery. Main crops are rice, grains and nuts.

NIGERIA

Land area 923,768 sq km (356,669 sq mi)
Major physical features highest point: Dimiong 2,042 m (6,700 ft); longest river: Niger (part) 4,200 km (2,600 mi)
Population (1994) 92,800,000
Form of government federal republic with military government
Largest cities Lagos (1,097,000); Ibadan (1,060,000); Abuja (capital – 378,671)
Official language English
Ethnic composition Hausa 21.3%; Yoruba 21.3%; Ibo 18.0%; Fulani 11.2%; Ibibio 5.6%; Kanuri 4.2%; Edo 3.4%; Tiv 2.2%; Ijaw 1.8%; Bura 1.7%; Nupe 1.2%; others 8.1%

Religious affiliations Muslim 45.0%; Protestant 26.3%; Roman Catholic 12.1%; African Christian 10.6%; others 6.0%
Currency 1 Nigerian naira = 100 kobo
Economy Gross national product (per capita 1993) US $300; Gross domestic product (1993) US $31,344 million
Life expectancy at birth male 51.0 yr; female 54.0 yr
Major resources petroleum, cocoa, rubber, tin, coal, iron ore, palm kernals, groundnuts (peanuts), fisheries
Major international organizations OPEC, UN, UNESCO, WHO

Nigeria is the largest country on the coast of west Africa, and the most populous on the continent. It is home to over 200 peoples, but inter-ethnic strife has dominated politics since an Ibo coup in 1966. The discovery of petroleum has boosted the economy.

NORTH KOREA

Land area 122,400 sq km (47,300 sq mi)
Major physical features highest point: Mount Paektu 2,744 m (9,003 ft); longest river: Yalu 810 km (503 mi)
Population (1994) 23,066,573
Form of government one-party republic with one legislative house
Largest cities P'yongyang (capital – 2,639,000); Hamhung (775,000); Ch'ongjin (754,000)
Official language Korean
Ethnic composition Korean 99.8%; Chinese 0.2%

Religious affiliations nonreligious 67.9%; traditional beliefs 15.6%; Ch'ondogyo 13.9%; Buddhist 1.7%; Christian 0.9%
Currency 1 won (Wn) = 100 chon
Economy Gross national product (per capita) 1993 US $1,390
Life expectancy at birth male 66.7 yr; female 73.0 yr
Major resources iron ore, coal, lead, tungsten, zinc
Major international organizations IMF (observer), NAM, UN, UNESCO, WHO

The Communist republic of North Korea occupies the northern half of the Korean peninsula on the northeastern coast of Asia. It is half of a nation that was partitioned during the years following World War II; South Korea is a non-Communist state with a free-market economy. The North Korean economy depends on manufacturing heavy machinery and mining, and a high percentage of food products have to be imported. More than 90% of this command economy is socialized, and all agricultural land is collectivized.

NORWAY

Land area   323,878 sq km (125,050 sq mi)
Major physical features   highest point: Glittertind 2,470 m (8,104 ft); longest river: Glåma 610 km (380 mi)
Population   (1994) 4,315,000
Form of government   multiparty constitutional monarchy with one legislative house
Largest cities   Oslo (capital – 683,000); Bergen (213,000); Trondheim (138,000)
Ethnic composition   Norwegian 95.8%; other Scandinavians 1.0%; others 3.2%

Currency   1 krone (NKr) = 100 øre
Economy   Gross national product (per capita 1993) US $25,970; Gross domestic product (1993) US $103,419,000
Life expectancy at birth   male 74.0 yr; female 80.9 yr
Major resources   petroleum, natural gas, timber, minerals, fish, hydroelectric power
Major international organizations   Council of Europe, EFTA, GATT, IMF, NATO, OECD, UN, UNESCO, WHO

Norway's economy is characterized by high taxes, full social benefits and continuing low unemployment. Its voters narrowly rejected membership of the European Union in 1994.

OMAN

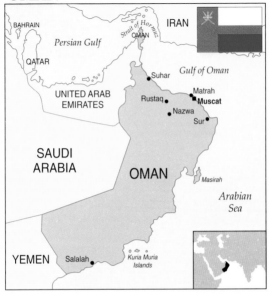

Land area 300,000 sq km (116,000 sq mi)

Major physical feature highest point: Jabal Akhdar 3,018 m (9,902 ft)

Population (1994) 1,701,000

Form of government absolute monarchy with one appointed council

Capital city Muscat (250,000)

Official language Arabic

Ethnic composition Omani Arab 73.5%; Indian 15.0%; others 11.5%

Official religion Islam

Currency 1 rial (RO) = 1,000 baiza

Economy Gross national product (per capita 1993) US $4,850; Gross domestic product (1993) US $11,686 million

Life expectancy at birth male 65.9 yr; female 69.8 yr

Major resources mining (petroleum), fish

Major international organizations AL, UN

Oman is one of the largest of the Persian Gulf states, but the economy is still developing. Petroleum products are the main revenue earners, with some tourism since the 1980s. The sultan, Qaboos bin Said, is comparatively liberal and although the media remains state-controlled, education and opportunities for women have improved.

PAKISTAN

Land area 796,095 sq km (307,374 sq mi)
Major physical features highest point: K2 8,611 m (28,250 ft); longest river: Indus 2,900 km (1,800 mi)
Population (1994) 128,856,000
Form of government federal multiparty republic with two legislative houses
Largest cities Islamabad (capital – 204,000); Karachi (5,181,000)
Official languages Urdu, English
Ethnic composition Punjabi 48.2%; Pashto 13.1%; Sindhi 11.8%; Urdu 7.6%; others 19.3%
Currency 1 rupee (PRe) = 100 paisa
Economy Gross national product (per capita 1993) US $430; Gross domestic product (1993) US $46,360 million
Life expectancy at birth male 56.8 yr; female 58 yr
Major resources natural gas, low-grade coal, iron ore, copper, salt, cotton, rice
Major international organizations Colombo Plan, Commonwealth, UN

Pakistan was created in 1947 out of several former territories of British-ruled India; it became a republic in 1956. Territorial disputes led to three wars with India, during which Pakistan developed nuclear weapons. In 1993, the military forced the president and prime minister out of office; but Prime Minister Benazir Bhutto was subsequently re-elected by democratic processes. The economy is growing quickly, but so is the population, most of which remains poor. Pakistan receives substantial foreign aid.

PALAU

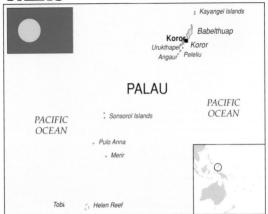

Land area 1,632 sq km (630 sq mi)
Major physical features 26 islands and over 300 islets; largest island is Babelthuap
Population (1994) 16,366
Form of government constitutional republic with two legislative houses
Capital city Koror (10,493); a new capital is being built in eastern Babelthuap
Official languages Palauan, English

Ethnic composition Japanese, Spanish, indigenous, Filipino
Religious affiliations Christian (Roman Catholic, Seventh-Day Adventists, protestant); one third follow the indigenous Modekngei beliefs
Currency U.S. currency is used
Major resources fish, shipping, tourism
Major international organizations UN

The republic of Palau, also known by its native name Belau, in the western Pacific Ocean became an independent republic in October 1994. Before that time it was a UN trusteeship in free association with the United States. The territory comprises the westernmost portion of the Caroline Islands chain some 850 km (528 mi) southeast of the Philippines. The main islands are part of a coralline reef structure on a volcanic base, with over 300 islets surrounding a huge central lagoon. The islands vary geologically from the high mountainous main island of Babelthuap to low coral islands fringed by barrier reefs. The reefs are home to a wide variety of marine life, and the hot wet climate supports lush vegetation. Agriculture and fishing remain at subsistence level, though some tuna is exported and copra is grown as a cash crop. Coconut oil is also exported in small quantities. Transportation is mainly by sea or air, and tourism has not been developed in the republic.

PANAMA

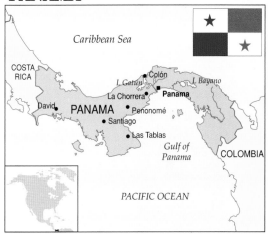

Land area 77,082 sq km (29,762 sq mi)
Major physical features highest point:
Volcán Barú 3,475 m (11,400 ft)
Population (1994) 2,630,000
Form of government multiparty republic
with one legislative house
Capital city Panama (853,000)
Official language Spanish
Ethnic composition mestizo 62%; black 14%;
white 10%; Amerindian 6%; others 8%
Religious affiliations Roman Catholic 84.0%;

Protestant 4.8%; Muslim 4.5%; others 6.7%
Currency 1 balboa (B) = 100 centesimos
Economy Gross national product (per capita
1993) US $2,600; Gross domestic product
(1993) US $6,565 million
Life expectancy at birth male 72.3 yr;
female 77.6 yr
Major resources bananas, shrimp, sugar,
coffee, timber (mahogany)
Major international organizations IBRD,
NAM, OAS, UN, UNESCO, WHO

Panama, on the land bridge connecting North and South America, has had particular international significance since the Panama Canal (linking the Atlantic and the Pacific via the Caribbean) was opened in 1914. Although under United States control for much of this century, the Canal zone, a site of high industrial development, reverted to Panama in 1979, and control of the canal itself is due to be relinquished by the US in the year 2000. Panama's financial services are expanding, but foreign investment is low due to political instability. In 1989 the United States invaded Panama and overthrew its military dictator, General Noriega, who was tried and imprisoned for drug smuggling. The army was disbanded and free elections were held in 1989 and 1994.

PAPUA NEW GUINEA

Land area 462,840 sq km (178,703 sq mi)
Major physical features highest point: Mount Wilhelm 4,508 m (14,790 ft); longest river: Sepik about 1,000 km (600 mi)
Population (1994) 4,197,000
Form of government multiparty constitutional monarchy with one legislative house
Capital city Port Moresby (174,000)
Official language English, but it is not widely spoken; there are 715 local languages
Ethnic composition Papuan 84%; Melanesian 15%; others (Micronesian, Polynesian, Negrito) 1%

Religious affiliations Protestant 56%; Roman Catholic 22%; traditional beliefs 22.%
Currency 1 kina (K) = 100 toea
Economy Gross national product (per capita 1993) US $1,130; Gross domestic product (1993) US $5,091 million
Life expectancy at birth male 55.6 yr; female 57.3
Major resources gold, silver, copper, natural gas, timber; possible petroleum reserves
Major international organizations ASEAN, IBRD, NAM, UN, UNESCO, WHO

Papua New Guinea shares the Pacific island of New Guinea with Indonesia. Exploitation of its mineral resources has been hampered by rough terrain and local unrest.

PARAGUAY

Land area 406,752 sq km (157,048 sq mi)
Major physical feature highest point:
Caaguazú Mountains 700 m (2,300 ft)
Population (1994) 5,214,000
Form of government multiparty republic
with two legislative houses
Largest cities Asunción (capital – 729,000);
Ciudad del Este (110,000)
Official language Spanish
Ethnic composition mestizo 90.8%;
Amerindian 3.0%; German 1.7%; others 4.5%
Official religion Roman Catholicism

Currency 1 guarani (G) = 100 céntimos
Economy Gross national product (per capita
1993) US $1,510; Gross domestic product
(1993) US $6,825 million
Life expectancy at birth male 71.7 yr;
female 74.9 yr
Major resources timber, hydroelectric
power, agriculture, some minerals (iron ore,
limestone, manganese)
Major international organizations GATT,
IBRD, IMF, OAS, UN, UNESCO, WHO

Paraguay is a small landlocked country in South America, sandwiched between
Argentina, Bolivia and Brazil. The world's largest hydroelectric project (shared with
Brazil) has made Paraguay an electricity exporter, but the economy remains mostly
agricultural and confined to the populated eastern region. Economic growth was erratic
in the 1980s due to bad weather and low export prices for cash crops. After 60 years of
military rule Paraguay held free elections for the first time in 1989.

PERU

Land area 1,285,216 sq km (496,225 sq mi)
Major physical feature highest point:
Huascarán 6,768 m (22,205 ft)
Population (1994) 23,651,000
Form of government multiparty republic
Largest cities Lima (capital – 6,415,000);
Arequipa (635,000); Trujillo (532,000)
Official languages Spanish, Quechua
Ethnic composition Quechua 45%;
mestizo 37%; white 15%; others 3%
Official religion Roman Catholicism

Currency 1 neuvo sol (S/.) = 100 céntimos
Economy Gross national product (per capita
1993) US $1,490; Gross domestic product
(1993) US $41,061 million
Life expectancy at birth male 63.4 yr;
female 67.9 yr
Major resources gold, silver, copper, petro-
leum, timber, fish, iron ore, coal, phosphate
Major international organizations GATT,
IBRD, IMF, NAM, OAS, UN, UNESCO, WHO

Civil unrest is a problem throughout Peru. Despite a wealth of natural resources, the
economy is struggling under massive foreign debt. President Alberto Fujimori staged a
coup against himself in 1992 to obtain wider powers to fight the national terrorist group
Sendero Luminoso (Shining Path). Widespread privatization of industry is underway.

PHILIPPINES

Land area 300,000 sq km (115,800 sq mi)
Major physical features largest island:
Luzon, 104,684 sq km (40,419 sq mi); highest
point: Mount Apo, 2,954 m (9,692 ft)
Population (1994) 65,000,000
Form of government multiparty republic
with two legislative houses
Largest cities Manila (capital – 7,832,000);
Quezon City (1,587,000)
Official languages Pilipino, English
Ethnic composition Talalog 29.7%; Cebuano
24.2%; Ilocano 10.3%; Hiligayon Ilongo 9.2%;
Bicol 5.6%; Samar-Leyte 4%; others 17%

Religious affiliations Roman Catholic 84.1%;
Muslim 4.3%; Protestant 3.9%; others 7.7%
Currency 1 peso (P) = 100 centavos
Economy Gross national product (per capita
1993) US $850; Gross domestic product
(1993) US $54,068 million
Life expectancy at birth male 63 yr;
female 70 yr
Major resources nickel, copper, gold, fish,
rice, tobacco, pineapples, sugar, timber
Major international organizations ASEAN,
GATT, IBRD, IMF, NAM, UN, UNESCO UNHCR,
WHO

The Philippines comprises over 7,000 islands off the southeast coast of Asia. Current
economic policy is to promote political stability to allow industry to develop.

POLAND

Land area 312,683 sq km (120,727 sq mi)
Major physical features highest point: Rysy
(Tatra Mountains) 2,499 m (8,187 ft); longest
river: Vistula 1,086 km (675 mi)
Population (1990) 38,655,000
Form of government multiparty republic
with two legislative houses
Largest cities Warsaw (capital – 1,655,000);
Lodz (852,000); Kracow (748,000)
Official language Polish
Ethnic composition Polish 97.6%; German
1.3%; Ukrainian 0.6%; Belarus 0.5%

Religious affiliations Roman Catholic 95%
Currency 1 zloty (Zl) = 100 groszy
Economy Gross national product (per capita
1993) US $2,260; Gross domestic product
(1993) US $85,853 million
Life expectancy at birth male 68.6 yr;
female 76.9 yr
Major resources natural gas, coal, lead,
silver, sulfur, copper, salt, rye, potatoes
Major international organizations GATT,
IBRD, IMF, NAM, UN, UNESCO, WHO

Poland is a flat open country in central Europe and has been conquered many times by
other nations. It was the first country invaded by Hitler at the beginning of World War II
and was occupied by the Soviets from 1945. In 1989 Poland was the first country to
break through the iron curtain. A non-Communist government was formed in that year,
following a series of strikes by *Solidarity*, a trade union that became a political party.
Its leader, Lech Walesa, was elected president in 1990. Economic reform followed,
assisted by write-offs of Poland's huge foreign debt. The free market is now flourishing,
but industrial pollution is a major problem.

PORTUGAL

Land area 92,389 sq km (35,672 sq mi)

Major physical features highest point: (Azores) Ponta do Pico 2,351 m (7,713 ft); longest river: Tagus (part) 1,010 km (630 mi)

Population (1994) 10,524,000

Form of government multiparty republic with one legislative house

Largest cities Lisbon (capital – 678,000); Oporto (311,000)

Official language Portuguese

Ethnic composition Portuguese 99.1%

Religious affiliations Roman Catholic 97 %

Currency 1 escudo (Esc) = 100 centavos

Economy Gross national product (per capita 1993) US $9,130; Gross domestic product (1993) US $85,665 million

Life expectancy at birth male 71.8 yr; female 78.9 yr

Major resources fish, wine, cork, marble, tungsten, iron ore, uranium ore, tourism

Major international organizations EU, GATT, IBRD, NAM, NATO, UN, UNESCO, WHO

Portugal, the western neighbor of Spain, was once a wealthy naval power with colonies in Brazil, India (Goa) and China. (Macao, the last of the colonies, will return to Chinese ownership in 1999). From the early 19th century Portugal was in decline, and suffered under dictatorships from 1926–75. It joined the EC in 1986, and though it is not yet prosperous by European standards, its stability and low prices make it a popular tourist destination. Further economic development depends on a recovered European market.

QATAR

Land area 11,400 sq km (4,400 sq mi)
Population (1994) 513,000
Form of government monarchy
Capital city Doha (217,000)
Official language Arabic
Ethnic composition Arab 40.0%; Indian 18.0%; Pakistani 18.0%; Iranian 10.0%; others 14.0%
Religious affiliations Muslim 92.4%; Christian 5.9%; Hindu 1.1%; others 0.6%

Official religion Islam
Currency 1 Qatari riyal (QR) = 100 dirhams
Economy Gross national product (per capita 1993) US $16,000
Life expectancy at birth male 70.1 yr; female 75.1 yr
Major resources petroleum, natural gas, fish
Major international organizations AL, IBRD, IMF, NAM, OPEC, UN, WHO

The small peninsular kingdom of Qatar is on the southern edge of the Persian Gulf, at the tip of the Arabian Peninsula. The present Amir seized power in a bloodless coup in 1972, and has designated his son as successor. Although the royal family has ruled continuously since the 18th century, Qatar was controlled by the British before becoming independent in 1981, when it chose not to join the neighboring United Arab Emirates. Qatar's prosperity is completely dependent on huge deposits of petroleum and natural gas. It was a founding member of OPEC, and now enjoys a per capita income on a level with the wealthiest countries in the developed world. Like Kuwait, Qatar has a disproportionately high number of foreign workers. In spite of the predominance of the conservative Wahhabi Muslim faith, a relatively tolerant society exists, with freedom of worship for non-Muslims. Women are permitted to appear unveiled in public.

ROMANIA

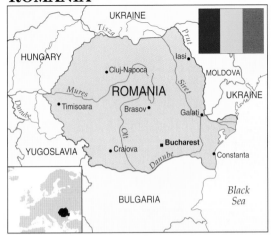

Land area 237,500 sq km (91,699 sq mi)
Major physical features highest point: Mount Negoiu 2,548 m (8,360 ft); longest river: Danube (part) 2,850 km (1,770 mi)
Population (1994) 23,181,000
Form of government multiparty republic with two legislative houses
Largest cities Bucharest (capital – 2,217,000); Brasov (364,000)
Official language Romanian
Ethnic composition Romanian 89.1%; Hungarian 8.9%; German 0.4%; others 1.6%

Religious affiliations Romanian Orthodox 70%; none 16%; Greek Orthodox 10%; others 4%
Currency 1 leu (L – plural lei) = 100 bani
Economy Gross national product (per capita 1993) US $1,140; Gross domestic product (1993) US $25,969 million
Life expectancy at birth male 68.8 yr; female 74.8 yr
Major resources petroleum, natural gas, timber, coal, salt, iron ore, cereals
Major international organizations BSEC, EBRD, GATT, NAM, UN, WHO

Romania, in southeastern Europe on the Black Sea coast, borders the former Soviet Union, and has spent most of its recent history in the shadow of its powerful neighbor. During the period 1965–89 Romania suffered under the dark and repressive rule of Soviet-backed dictator Nicolae Ceausescu who was eventually overthrown and executed following a popular revolt. Today it is facing the enormous task of economic reform, but without a skilled workforce and with the handicaps of massive inflation and unemployment. A black market in basic foodstuffs flourishes. Despite rich natural resources, fuel and raw materials for industry continue to be imported.

RUSSIA

The Russian Federation (Russia) is the leading member of the Commonwealth of Independent States, the 22 republics that comprise the vast majority of the former Soviet Union. It is nearly twice the size of either China or the United States, and is almost unimaginably rich in natural resources, including precious metals, petroleum and natural gas. However, the transition from a centrally-planned economy to the free market, which predated the establishment of the CIS in 1991, has resulted in corruption and increasingly uneven distribution of wealth, as well as high inflation. The lack of stability in the economy was a prime factor that contributed to the dissolution of the Soviet Union under its last Communist leader, Mikhail Gorbachev. As industry has been denationalized, output has dropped, and many officials and senior managers have resorted to stripping assets and depositing their money abroad. Smuggling and organized crime are rampant; the police can no longer provide effective protection from the various Russian 'mafias', whose leaders are Russia's richest citizens. Funding has been severely cut away from education and health, transport, the arts, and scientific research.

With the loss of state funding has gone much national pride, opening the way for ultra-right movements that promise to restore Russian prestige and crack down on crime. It has great popular appeal in the face of the failure of Russian president Boris Yeltsin to cope with the overwhelming post-independence problems. Many of the natural resources that Russia traditionally depended on are shared with other CIS republics, leading to conflict over ownership. To maintain control, Russia imposes strict limits on foreign investment in its own industries, and these are underexploited as a result.

Land area 17,075,400 sq km (6,592,800 sq mi)

Major physical features highest point: Elbrus 5,633 m (18,481 ft); longest river: Yenisey 5,870 km (3,650 mi)

Population (1994) 149,609,000

Form of government federal multiparty republic with two legislative houses

Largest cities Moscow (capital – 8,881,000); St. Petersburg (Leningrad, 4,467,000); Nizhni Novgorod (Gorky, 1,443,000); Novosibirsk (1,443,000); Yekaterinburg (Sverdlovsk, 1,375,000); Samara (Kuybyshev, 1,258,000); Omsk (1,159,000); Chelyabinsk (1,148,000); Kazan (1,103,000)

Official language Russian

Ethnic composition Russian 81.5%; Tatar 3.8%; Ukrainian 3.0%; Chuvash 1.2%; Bashkir 0.9%; Belarus 0.8%; others 8.8%

Religious affiliations Russian Orthodox; nonreligious; Jewish; Muslim; Buddhist

Currency 1 ruble (R) = 100 kopecks

Economy Gross national product (per capita 1993) US $2,340; Gross domestic product (1993) US $329,432 million

Life expectancy at birth male 63.8 yr; female 74.2 yr

Major resources oil, natural gas, coal, iron ore, platinum, copper, lead, zinc, tin, gold, silver, diamonds, timber, wheat, rye, barley, oats, flax, sugar beet, meat, milk, vegetables, manufacturing

Major international organizations BSEC, CIS, CSCE, EBRD, IMF, UN (Security Council), UNESCO, UNPROFOR, WHO

Administrative divisions within the Federation

21 Republics, 6 Territories, 49 Provinces, 11 Autonomous Areas, 2 Federal Cities.

REPUBLICS (with populations for 1994)

Adygeya	(449,000)	Karelia	(794,200)
Alania	(650,400)	Khakassia	(584,000)
Altai	(198,300)	Komi	(1,228,100)
Bashkortostan	(4,055,300)	Mari El	(764,700)
Buryatia	(1,052,800)	Mordovia	(962,700)
Chechenia	(1,308,000)*	Sakha	(1,197,760)
Chuvashia	(1,359,000)	Tatarstan	(3,743,600)
Dagestan	(1,953,000)	Tuva	(306,300)
Ingushetia	see Chechenia	Udmurtia	(1,640,700)
Kabardino-Balkaria	(785,800)°		
Kalmykia	(320,600)		
Karachai-Cherkessia	(434,100)		

* figures for 1992 only, includes Ingushetia

° figures for 1991 only

B.	BASHKORTOSTAN		
CH.	CHELYABINSK		
C.	CHUVASHIA		
IV.	IVANOVO		
K.	KALININGRAD		
KA.	KALUGA		
KH.	KHAKASSIA		
K.P.	KOMI-PERMYAK		
KO.	KOSTROMA		
L.	LIPETSK		
MA.	MARI EL		
MO.	MORDOVIA		
M.	MOSCOW		
N.	NIZHNI NOVGOROD		
O.	OREL		
R.	RYAZAN		
S.	STAVROPOL		
T.	TAMBOV		
U.	ULYANOVSK		
US.	UST-ORDYN-BURYAT		
V.	VLADIMIR		
VO.	VORONEZH		
Y.	YAROSLAVL		

Administrative divisions (cont)

TERRITORIES (KRAI)	PROVINCES (OBLAST)	Irkutsk	Kursk
Altai	Amur	Ivanovo	Lipetsk
Khabarovsk	Arkhangel	Kaliningrad	Magadan
Krasnodar	Astrakhan	Kaluga	Moscow
Krasnoyarsk	Belgorod	Kamchatka	Murmansk
Primorye	Bryansk	Kemerovo	Nizhni Novgorod
Stavropol	Chelyabinsk	Kirov	Novgorod
	Chita	Kostroma	Novosibirsk
		Kurgan	Omsk

Orel	Smolensk	Voronezh	Koryak
Orenburg	Sverdlovsk	Yaroslavl	Nenets
Penza	Tambov		Taimyr
Perm	Tomsk	**AUTONOMOUS**	Ust-Ordyn-Buryat
Pskov	Tula	**AREAS**	Yamalo-Nenets
Rostov	Tver	**Agin-Buryat**	
Ryazan	Tyumen	Birobijan	**FEDERAL CITIES**
St. Petersburg	Ulyanovsk	Chukot	**Moscow**
Sakhalin	Vladimir	Evenki	**St. Petersburg**
Samara	Volgograd	Khanty-Mansi	
Saratov	Vologda	Komi-Permyak	

RWANDA

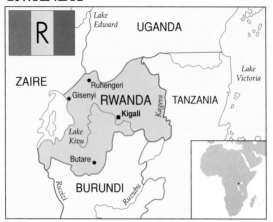

Land area   26,338 sq km (10,169 sq mi)
Major physical features   highest point:
Mount Karisimbi 4,507 m (14,786 ft)
Population   (1994) 8,374,000
Form of government   transitional government working toward democratic elections
Capital city   Kigali (233,000)
Official languages   Kinyarwanda, French
Ethnic composition   Hutu 90.0%; Tutsi 9.0%;
Twa Pygmy 1.0%
Religious affiliations   Roman Catholic 65%;
traditional 17%; Protestant 9%; Muslim 9%
Currency   franc (RF) = 100 centimes
Economy   Gross national product (per capita 1993) US $210; Gross domestic product (1993) US $1,359 million
Life expectancy at birth   male 39.3 yr;
female 41.2 yr
Major resources   coffee, tea, gold, tin ore,
tungsten ore, natural gas, hydroelectricity
Major international organizations   GATT,
IMF, NAM, OAU, UN, UNESCO, WHO

Rwanda, a small landlocked state in central Africa, is one of the poorest and most densely populated countries in the world. A former colony of Germany and then Belgium, it became independent in 1962. Conflict between Hutus and Tutsis has been frequent, notably in 1963 and 1990, when neighboring Burundian and exiled Tutsis invaded. In 1994 war erupted after the death of the president in a plane crash. More than 200,000 people are estimated to have died, and the United Nations voted to set up a tribunal to try crimes of genocide. The fragile economy is mainly agricultural, established through numerous smallholdings on hillsides that suffer badly from erosion. Recently the scant economic structures that existed have been disrupted by the mass movement of refugees, and Rwanda is now dependent on foreign aid.

178

SAINT KITTS-NEVIS

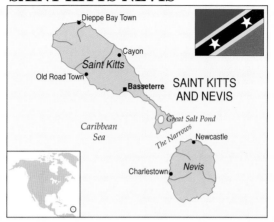

Land area 269 sq km (104 sq mi)

Major physical feature highest point: Mount Misery 1,156 m (3,793 ft)

Population (1994) 40,671

Form of government multiparty constitutional monarchy with one legislative house

Capital city Basseterre (15,000)

Official language English

Ethnic composition black 90.5%; mixed 5.0%; Indian 3.0%; white 1.5%

Religious affiliations Anglican 32.6%; Methodist 28.8%; other Protestants 21.3%; Roman Catholic 7.2%; others 10.1%

Currency 1 East Caribbean dollar (EC$) = 100 cents

Economy Gross national product (per capita 1991) US $3,960; Gross domestic product (1993) US $185 million

Life expectancy at birth male 63.1 yr; female 69.3 yr

Major resources sugar, cotton, salt, fish, tourism

Major international organizations CARICOM, ECLAC, IBRD, IMF, LORCS, UN, UNCTAD, UNESCO, WHO

The Federation of Saint Kitts and Nevis in the eastern Caribbean is part of the Leeward Islands of the Antilles. It became independent from the United Kingdom in 1983. The islands have limited resources; even their output of sugar cane, the most important cash crop, is low compared with larger islands. Remittances from overseas workers are significant, and the islands receive international aid. Tourism aimed at the mass market in the United States has been developed, and there is potential for expanding the fishing industry. Other significant industries are clothing, footware and beverages for export. In 1992, in spite of worldwide recession, the economy was growing by about 4 percent.

SAINT LUCIA

Land area   617 sq km (238 sq mi)

Major physical feature   highest point: Mount Gimie 959 m (3,145 ft)

Population   (1994) 145,000

Form of government   multiparty constitutional monarchy with two legislative houses

Capital city   Castries (56,000)

Official language   English

Ethnic composition   black 87.0%; mixed 9.1%; Indian 2.6%; white 1.3%

Religious affiliations   Roman Catholic 90.0%; Protestant 7.0%; others 3.0%

Currency   1 East Caribbean dollar (EC$) = 100 cents

Economy   Gross national product (per capita 1991) US $2,500; Gross domestic product (1993) US $433 million

Life expectancy at birth   male 67.1 yr; female 71.8 yr

Major resources   timber, bananas, mineral springs, pumice, tourism

Major international organizations   CARICOM, ECLAC, GATT, IBRD, IMF, NAM, UN, UNCTAD, UNESCO, WHO

The Caribbean island of St. Lucia, one of the Windward islands of the Antilles, gained independence from the United Kingdom in 1979. The beauty of the island attracts many tourists, and it is an important stop for cruise ships. There is an increasing need to protect St. Lucia's remaining rainforest from development. Bananas have replaced sugar cane as the chief export crop. Most other agriculture is at subsistence level, and food has to be imported. There are plans to harness geothermal energy from the hot mineral springs to lessen dependence on imported energy. Crime and unemployment are low, and the economy is growing rapidly, driven by tourism and foreign investment in manufacturing and data processing.

ST. VINCENT & THE GRENADINES

Land area 389 sq km (150 sq mi)
Major physical features highest point: Soufrière 1,234 m (4,048 ft); largest island: Saint Vincent 347 sq km (134 sq mi)
Population (1994) 115,000
Form of government multiparty constitutional monarchy with one legislative house
Capital city Kingstown (27,000)
Official language English
Ethnic composition black 74.0%; mulatto 19.0%; white 3.0%; black Carib 2.0%; Asian Indian 2.0%

Religious affiliations Anglican 36.0%; Protestants 41.3%; Roman Catholic 19.3%; others 3.4%
Currency 1 East Caribbean dollar (EC$) = 100 cents
Economy Gross national product (per capita 1992) US $2,000
Life expectancy at birth male 70.8 yr; female 73.8 yr
Major resources bananas, tourism, arrowroot
Major international organizations CARICOM, ECLAC, GATT, IMF, UN, UNESCO, WHO

St. Vincent and the Grenadines comprise more than a dozen islands in the Windward group in the eastern Caribbean. St. Vincent is the largest of the islands. Another, Mustique, is an exclusive holiday island; a third, Union Island, is being developed as a major center for yachting holidays. St. Vincent is the world's leading producer of arrowroot starch and exports its cash crop of bananas, but there there is little other industry in the region. In spite of a wealth of jobs associated with tourism, unemployment among the native population is high – about 40 percent. The port at Kingstown is home to a merchant marine of more than 500 ships, but about 20 percent are foreign-owned; St. Vincent is a flag of convenience registry.

SAN MARINO

Land area 61 sq km (24 sq mi)

Major physical feature highest point: Monte Titano 739 m (2,424 ft)

Population (1994) 24,000

Form of government multiparty republic with one legislative house

Capital city San Marino (4,000)

Official language Italian

Ethnic composition Sammarinesi 84.9%; Italian 14.6%; others 0.5%

Religious affiliations Roman Catholic 95.2%; nonreligious 3.0%; others 1.8%

Currency 1 Italian lira (Lit) = 100 centesimi

Economy Gross national product (per capita 1992) US $9,000

Life expectancy at birth male 77.2 yr; female 85.3 yr

Major resources stone, wine, olives, tourism

Major international organizations CSCE, IMF, NAM, UN, UNCTAD, UNESCO, WHO

The landlocked state of San Marino in central Italy is the third smallest country in Europe (after the Vatican City and Monaco), and has been independent since it was founded in the 4th century. The state constitution dates back to 1600. San Marino declined to become part of Italy in 1861, though the economic and cultural links between the two have remained strong. Most of San Marino's raw materials for light industry (typically clothing, electronics and ceramics) come from Italy, as does its electric power supply. San Marino uses Italian currency, and sends many of its students to Italian universities. Tourism accounts for more than half of the gross national product and, surprisingly, more than 80 percent of tourists to San Marino are Italians. Unemployment in the state is low, and the standard of living is comparable to that of its larger neighbor. Women could not vote until 1960, nor hold office until 1973.

SÃO TOMÉ & PRÍNCIPE

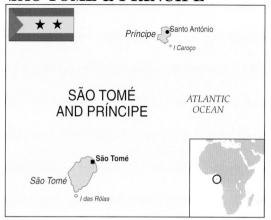

Land area 1,001 sq km (386 sq mi)

Major physical features highest point: Pico de Tomé 2,024 m (6,640 ft); largest island: São Tomé 859 sq km (332 sq mi)

Population (1994) 137,000

Form of government multiparty republic with one legislative house

Capital city São Tomé (35,000)

Official language Portuguese

Ethnic composition African (mainly Fang) 90%; Portuguese and Creole 10%

Religious affiliations Roman Catholic 84.0%; Protestant and others 16.0%

Currency 1 dobra (Db) = 100 cêntimos

Economy Gross national product (per capita 1991) US $350

Life expectancy at birth male 61.5 yr; female 65.2 yr

Major resources cocoa, fish

Major international organizations AfDB, ECA, IBRD, IMF, NAM, OAU, UN, UNCTAD, UNESCO, WHO

The islands of São Tomé & Príncipe, some 300 km (186 mi) off the west coast of Africa along the Equator, were Portuguese territories used as a penal colony and as a place of exile for deported Jews. Early sugar plantations on the islands were run by slave labor. Slavery was abolished in the 19th century, and following independence in 1975, São Tomé & Príncipe adopted a one-party Marxist system. At this point most of the several thousand Portuguese descendents left the country, which is now run by the black majority. A multiparty democratic system was introduced in 1990, sweeping away the Communist system of government. Declining production of cocoa (the chief crop) has led to a falling balance of payments and today overseas aid supplements the economy. Malnutrition is a common problem, and unemployment is widespread.

SAUDI ARABIA

Land area 2,240,000 sq km (865,000 sq mi)
Major physical feature highest point: Jabal Sawda 3,133 m (10,279 ft)
Population (1994) 18,197,000
Form of government monarchy
Largest cities Riyadh (capital – 2,000,000); Jedda (1,400,000); Mecca (618,000)
Official language Arabic
Ethnic composition Saudi 82.0%; Yemeni 9.6%; other Arabs 3.4%; others 5.0%
Official religion Islam

Currency 1 Saudi riyal (SR) = 100 halalah
Economy Gross national product (per capita 1993) US $6,610; Gross domestic product (1993) US $121,530 million
Life expectancy at birth male 66.2 yr; female 69.6 yr
Major resources petroleum, natural gas, gold, iron ore, copper
Major international organizations AfDB, AL, IBRD, IMF, NAM, OAPEC, OPEC, UN, UNCTAD, UNESCO, WHO

Saudi Arabia, a desert kingdom that dominates the Arabian peninsula, has the world's largest oil reserves. In the Gulf War of 1990 an international coalition based in Saudi Arabia defeated Iraq (which had invaded Kuwait). There are more than 4 million skilled foreign workers, though visitors other than Muslim pilgrims are discouraged. Open worship outside the Muslim faith is banned, and women have few rights. Foreign aid and some domestic programs were cut back in the 1990s after lavish spending in the 1980s.

SENEGAL

Land area 196,722 sq km (75,955 sq mi)
Major physical features highest point: Futa Jalon (edge) 500 m (1,640 ft); longest river: Senegal (part) 1,633 km (1,015 mi)
Population (1994) 8,730,000
Form of government multiparty republic with one legislative house
Capital city Dakar (1,382,000)
Official language French
Ethnic composition African 97.4% (Wolof 36.2%; Fulani 17.8%; Serer 17.0%; Tukulor 9.7%; Dyola 8.1%; Mandingo 6.5%; Soninke 2.1%); Arab 1.0%; others 1.6%

Religious affiliations Sunni Muslim 92.0%; Roman Catholic 2.0%; traditional beliefs and others 6.0%
Currency 1 CFA franc (CFAF) = 100 centimes
Economy Gross national product (per capita 1993) US $750; Gross domestic product (1993) US $5,770 million
Life expectancy at birth male 55.1 yr; female 58.1 yr
Major resources fish, peanuts, phosphate, iron ore, petroleum, millet, rice, cotton
Major international organizations AfDB, GATT, IBRD, IMF, NAM, OAU, UN, WHO

Senegal lies on the central west coast of Africa and surrounds the tiny state of Gambia. It is heavily dependent on one major cash crop, groundnuts (peanuts), though diversification is being encouraged into exploiting its deposits of petroleum and iron ore.

SEYCHELLES

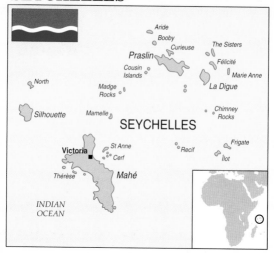

Land area 453 sq km (175 sq mi)
Major physical feature largest island:
Mahé 153 sq km (59 sq mi)
Population (1994) 72,000
Form of government one-party republic
with one legislative house
Capital city Victoria (24,000)
Official languages English, French, Creole
Ethnic composition Seychellois Creole
(Asian/African/European) 89.1%; Indian 4.7%;
Malagasy 3.1%; Chinese 1.6%; English 1.5%

Religious affiliations Roman Catholic 90.9%;
Protestant 7.5%; Hindu 0.7%; others 0.9%
Currency 1 rupee (SRe) = 100 cents
Economy Gross national product (per capita
1991) US $5,110
Life expectancy at birth male 66.0 yr;
female 73.4 yr
Major resources fish, cinnamon, copra,
tourism, coconuts, vanilla
Major international organizations AfDB,
ECA, IBRD, IMF, NAM, OAU, UN, WHO

The Seychelles consists of an archipelago of about 100 islands in the Indian Ocean off
the eastern central coast of Africa, northeast of Madagascar. They occupy a strategic
position on the sea route between Europe and India, and were French and British
colonies before attaining independence in 1976. Tourism is the mainstay of the economy,
employing about 30 percent of the workforce and providing nearly three-quarters of
hard currency earnings. Food processing and re-exported petroleum products are other
important industries. The standard of living is higher than in most African countries.

SIERRA LEONE

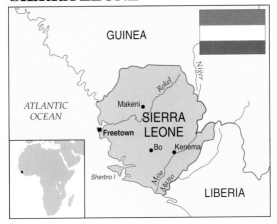

Land area 71,740 sq km (27,699 sq mi)
Major physical feature highest point:
Bintimani Peak 1,948 m (6,390 ft)
Population (1994) 4,630,000
Form of government one-party republic
with one legislative house
Capital city Freetown (470,000)
Official language English
Ethnic composition Mende 34.6%; Temne 31.7%;
Limba 8.4%; Kono 5.2%; Bullom 3.7%; Fulani
3.7%; Koranko 3.5%; Yalunka 3.5%; Kissi 2.3%;
others (Creole, European, Lebanese, Asian) 3.4%

Religious affiliations traditional beliefs 30%;
Sunni Muslim 60%; Protestant 6%; others 4%
Currency 1 leone (Le) = 100 cents
Economy Gross national product (per capita
1993) US $150; Gross domestic product (1993)
US $660 million
Life expectancy at birth male 43.6 yr;
female 42.6 yr
Major resources diamonds, titanium, gold,
bauxite, chromite, iron ore
Major international organizations AfDB,
GATT, IBRD, IDB, IMF, OAU, OIC, UN, WHO

Sierra Leone, on the northwest coast of Africa, is one of the poorest countries in the
world in spite of its diamond and gold mines. Founded in 1787 by the British as a colony
for freed slaves, it gained independence in 1961, and went bankrupt in 1978. A military
coup in 1992 re-imposed a one-party system after attempts to introduce a multiparty
democracy. Fighting with its neighbor Liberia and activity by rebels and bandits has disrupted even the subsistence agriculture that dominates the economy and prevented the
establishment of basic social and economic infrastructures. The potential for tourism
cannot be developed without stability. Average life expectancy is only 43 years, and only
21 percent of the population (11 percent of women) is literate.

SINGAPORE

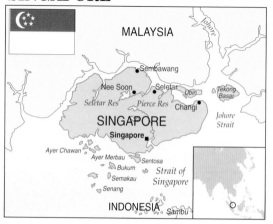

Land area 622 sq km (240 sq mi)

Major physical features highest point: Bukit Timah 176 m (581 ft)

Population (1994) 2,859,000

Form of government multiparty republic with one legislative house

Capital city Singapore (2,704,000)

Official languages Chinese, Malay, Tamil, English

Ethnic composition Chinese 76.4%; Malay 14.9%; Indian/Sri Lankan 6.4%; others 2.3%

Religious affiliations Buddhist 28.3%; Christian 18.7%; nonreligious 17.6%; Muslim 16.0%; Taoist 13.4%; Hindu 4.9%; others 1.1%

Currency 1 dollar (S$) = 100 cents

Economy Gross national product (per capita 1993) US $19,850; Gross domestic product (1993) US $55,153 million

Life expectancy at birth male 73.2 yr; female 79.0 yr

Major resources fish, deepwater ports, rubber, electronics, financial services

Major international organizations ASEAN, GATT, IBRD, IMF, NAM, UN, UNCTAD, WHO

Singapore, a tiny island in southeast Asia at the southern tip of the Malaysian peninsula, was established as a British trading post in 1819, was incorporated into Malaysia in 1963, and became independent in 1965. Today it is a highly prosperous and densely populated city state. Lacking natural resources, it has to import most of its food, energy and drinking water, but its financial services and high-tech industries are the backbone of a highly flexible modern economy. Inflation and unemployment are low, while the economy continues to grow. The workforce is supplemented by a significant number of foreign workers, mostly technical and scientific personnel. The population is almost entirely urban and is regulated by a strict code of behavior.

SLOVAKIA

Land area 49,035 sq km (18,932 sq mi)

Major physical features highest point: Gerlach Peak 2,665 m (8,743 ft); longest river: Vah 394 km (245 mi)

Population (1994) 5,404,000

Form of government parliamentary democracy

Capital city Bratislava (441,000)

Official language Slovak

Ethnic composition Slovak 85.6%; Hungarian 10.8%; Czech 1%; others 2.6%

Religious affiliations Roman Catholic 60.3%; nonreligious 9.7%; Protestant 8.4%; Orthodox 4.1%; other 17.5%

Currency 1 koruna (Sk) = 100 halierov

Economy Gross domestic product (1993) US $11,076 million

Life expectancy at birth male 68.6 yr; female 77.2 yr

Major resources lignite, iron ore, copper, manganese, salt, zinc, mineral springs

Major international organizations GATT, IBRD, IMF, NAM, UN, UNCTAD, WHO

The small landlocked state of Slovakia in central Europe was formed in 1993 from the southern half of Czechoslovakia, which had been under Communist rule since 1947. The economy was unevenly developed, with Slovakia having a smaller share of viable industries and infrastructure; it had produced mainly heavy goods and arms for the Eastern Bloc market that collapsed in the late 1980s. When the division occurred, much of the skilled workforce was concentrated in the new Czech Republic. Unemployment and inflation are high. There is potential for tourism if the infrastructure can be improved.

SLOVENIA

Land area 20,251 sq km (7,819 sq mi)
Major physical features highest point:
Triglav 2,864 m (9,393 ft); longest river: Sava
(part) 940 km (584 mi)
Population (1994) 1,972,000
Form of government multiparty republic
with two legislative houses
Largest cities Ljubljana (capital – 323,000);
Maribor (153,000); Kranj (72,814)
Official language Slovene
Ethnic composition (1994) Slovene 90.5%;
others (Serb, Croat, Italian, Austrian) 9.5%

Religious affiliations Roman Catholic
96.0%; Mulim 1.0%; others 3.0%
Currency 1 tolar (SlT) = 100 stotins
Economy Gross national product (per capita
1993) US $6,490; Gross domestic product
(1993) US $10,337 million
Life expectancy at birth male 70.5 yr;
female 78.4 yr
Major resources lignite coal, lead, zinc,
uranium, silver, mercury, manufacturing
Major international organizations EBRD,
IBRD, IMF, NAM, UN, UNCTAD, WHO

The central European republic of Slovenia declared independence from the former state
of Yugoslavia in 1991. Traditionally it has maintained closer ties to Austria and Italy
than to its Balkan neighbors, and has experienced no serious ethnic conflict in the
1990s, though it has taken in some Croatian and Bosnian refugees. Its relatively developed free-market economy has been disrupted in the short term by regional wars –
industrial production has fallen more than 25 percent. The IMF and the European Union
are aid donors, and Slovenia plans to apply for EU membership.

SOLOMON ISLANDS

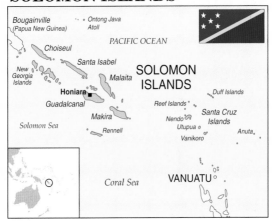

Land area 28,370 sq km (10,954 sq mi)

Major physical features largest island: Guadalcanal 5,336 sq km (2,060 sq mi); highest point: Makarakomburu 2,447 m (8,028 ft)

Population (1994) 386,000

Form of government multiparty constitutional monarchy with one legislative house

Capital city Honiara (Guadalcanal, 34,000)

Official language English

Ethnic composition Melanesian 94.2%; Polynesian 3.7%; other Pacific islanders 1.4%; European 0.4%; Asian 0.2%; others 0.1%

Religious affiliations Protestant 77.5%; Roman Catholic 19.2%; others 3.3%

Currency 1 Solomon Islands dollar = 100 cents

Economy Gross national product (per capita 1993) US $560

Life expectancy at birth male 68.0 yr; female 61.4 yr

Major resources fish, timber, copra; some minerals (gold, zinc, lead, nickel, phosphates)

Major international organizations IBRD, IMF, UN, WHO

The Solomon Islands are scattered through the South Pacific east of Papua New Guinea. They were the site of fierce fighting between Japanese and American forces in World War II (especially on Guadalcanal) and became independent from Britain in 1978. There is little arable land, but subsistence agriculture supports most of the population. The considerable mineral resources are undeveloped. Local environmental groups oppose the mining of bauxite, and the Solomons are trying to regain ownership of copper-rich Bougainville Island, now part of Papua New Guinea, which is geographically part of the Solomon Islands archipelago. A severe hurricane in 1986 destroyed much of the country's infrastructure, and the internal road system remains poor.

SOMALIA

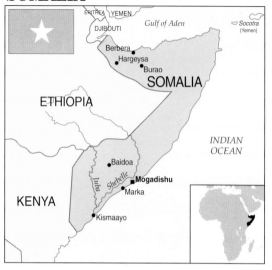

Land area 637,657 sq km (246,201 sq mi)

Major physical features highest point: Surud Ad 2,416 m (7,927 ft); longest river: Shebelle (part) 2,010 km (1,250 mi)

Population (1990) 6,667,000

Form of government one-party republic with one legislative house

Largest cities Mogadishu (capital – 1,000,000); Hargeysa (400,000); Burao (300,000) Baidoa (300,000)

Official language Somali

Ethnic composition Somali 85.0%; Arab 1.2%; Bantu 0.4%; others 13.4%

Religious affiliations Sunni Muslim 99.8%; Christian 0.1%; others 0.1%

Currency 1 Somali shilling = 100 cents

Economy Gross national product (per capita 1991) US $150; Gross domestic product (1991) US $835 million

Life expectancy at birth male 54.5yr; female 55.0 yr

Major resources livestock, bananas, uranium, iron ore, tin, gypsum, bauxite, copper

Major international organizations AfDB, AL, GATT, IBRD, IMF, NAM, OAU, UN, UNESCO, UNHCR, WHO

The northeast African country of Somalia is one of the poorest and least developed countries in the world. Half of the population are nomadic and live by raising livestock. The predominant agricultural sector and small industrial sector have been devastated by civil war. By 1991, 2.8 million war refugees were near starvation, with armed gangs stealing food and other aid. American troops were sent in to protect aid distribution.

SOUTH AFRICA

Land area 1,225,815 sq km (473,290 sq mi)
Population (1994) 40,435,000
Form of government multiparty republic
Capital cities Pretoria (administrative – 823,000); Bloemfontein (judicial – 233,000); Cape Town (legislative – 1,912,000)
Official languages Afrikaans, English, Ndebele, Sepedi, Setswana, Sesotho, Siswati, Tshivenda, Xhosa, Xitsonga, Zulu
Ethnic composition Zulu 23.8%; mixed race 10.5%; Afrikaans 10.2%; North Sotho 9.8%; Xhosa 9.7%; South Sotho 7.3%; English 6.5%; Tswana 5.7%; Asian 3.3%; others 13.2%
Religious affiliations Independent Black Christian 20.8%; Afrikaans Reformed 15.5%; Roman Catholic 9.6%; other Christians 32.2%; Hindu 2.1%; Muslim 1.4%; others 18.4%
Currency 1 rand (R) = 100 cents
Economy Gross national product (per capita 1993) US $2,980; Gross domestic product (1993) US $105,636 million
Life expectancy at birth male 62.3 yr; female 67.9 yr
Major resources gold, diamonds, platinum, natural gas, uranium, coal, other minerals
Major international organizations GATT, IBRD, IMF, OAU, UN, UNCTAD, WHO

South Africa is a large country at the tip of the African continent. For most of the 20th century the native black people were discriminated against by a system called apartheid, abolished in the early 1990s after years of international economic sanctions. In 1994 the newly enfranchised black voters elected Nelson Mandela to the presidency.

SOUTH KOREA

Land area 99,173 sq km (38,291 sq mi)
Major physical features highest point:
Halla-san (Cheju island), 1,950 m (6,398 ft);
longest river: Han, 470 km (292 mi)
Population (1994) 45,082,880
Form of government multiparty republic
Largest cities Seoul (capital – 10,628,000);
Pusan (3,798,000); Taegu (2,229,000)
Official language Korean
Ethnic composition Korean 99.9%; Chinese 0.1%
Religious affiliations Christianity 48.6%;
Buddhism 47.4%; others 4.0%

Currency 1 won (W) = 100 chon
Economy Gross national product (per capita
1993) US $7,660; Gross domestic product
(1993) US $330,831 million
Life expectancy at birth male 67.4 yr;
female 74.0 yr
Major resources coal, lead, tungsten, fish,
graphite, molybdenum, hydropower, electron-
ics, shipbuilding, automobiles, textiles
Major international organizations AfDB,
EBRD, GATT, IBRD, UN, UNCTAD, UNESCO,
WHO

South Korea occupies the southern part of the Korean peninsula in northeastern Asia.
The territory also includes the island of Cheju. In the late 1980s, South Korea had an
annual economic growth rate of more than 10 percent, and was known as an "economic
miracle". Today it is a market leader in shipbuilding and electronics. Tension continues
with North Korea, a single-party Communist state with a centrally planned economy.

SPAIN

Land area 504,750 sq km (94,885 sq mi)

Major physical features highest point: (Canaries) Pico de Teide 3,718 m (12,195 ft); longest river: Tagus (part) 1,010 km (630 mi)

Population (1994) 39,303,000

Form of government multiparty constitutional monarchy with two legislative houses

Capital city Madrid (3,121,000)

Official language Castilian Spanish

Ethnic composition Spanish 72.3%; Catalan 16.3%; Galician 8.1%; Basque 2.3%; others 1%

Religious affiliations Roman Catholic 97.0%; others 3.0%

Currency 1 peseta (Pta) = 100 céntimos

Economy Gross national product (per capita 1993) US $13,590; Gross domestic product (1993) US $478,582 million

Life expectancy at birth male 74.4 yr; female 81.2 yr

Major resources minerals, wine, olives, hydropower, tourism

Major international organizations AfDB, EU, GATT, IBRD, IMF, NAM, NATO, UN, WHO

Spain occupies the largest part of the Iberian Peninsula in western Europe. Since the 1950s, industry has been promoted to replace the traditional agricultural economy, and mass tourism in coastal resorts continues to be a major revenue earner.

SRI LANKA

Land area 65,610 sq km (25,332 sq mi)
Major physical features highest point: Pidurutalagala 2,518 m (8,261 ft); longest river: Mahaweli 329 km (206 mi)
Population (1994) 18,130,000
Form of government multiparty republic with one legislative house
Capital city Colombo (1,863,000)
Official languages Sinhala, Tamil
Ethnic composition Sinhalese 74.0%; Tamil 18.2%; Sri Lankan Moor 7.1%; others 0.7%
Religious affiliations Buddhist 69.3%; Hindu 15.5%; Muslim 7.6%; Christian 7.5%; others 0.1%
Currency 1 Sri Lanka rupee = 100 cents
Economy Gross national product (per capita 1993) US $600; Gross domestic product (1993) US $9,377 million
Life expectancy at birth male 69.4 yr; female 74.5 yr
Major resources tea, coconuts, rubber, limestone, graphite, mineral sands, gems, tourism
Major organizations GATT, IBRD, IMF, NAM, UN, UNCTAD, UNESCO, WHO

The island republic of Sri Lanka, off the southeastern coast of India, won independence from the UK in 1948. Once a popular tourist destination, it has been disrupted by civil war since 1983, triggered by the Tamil population who want to form their own state. The president was assassinated in 1993, and the Tamil rebels are believed to have been involved in the assassination of Indian president Rajiv Gandhi in the previous year. More recently violence on the island has decreased, and the economy has begun to recover, growing 5 percent in 1993. Industry (mostly textiles) has overtaken agriculture as the main source of export income. Literacy is high, and healthcare is free to all citizens.

SUDAN

Land area 2,503,890 sq km (966,757 sq mi)
Major physical features highest point: Kinyeti 3,187 m (10,450 ft); longest river: Nile (part) 6,690 km (4,160 mi)
Population (1994) 29,420,000
Form of government transitional republic; military government collapsed in 1993
Capital city Khartoum (561,000)
Official language Arabic
Ethnic composition Arab 49.1%; Dinka 11.5%; Nuba 8.1%; Beja 6.4%; Nuer 4.9%; Azande 2.7%; Bari 2.5%; Fur 2.1%; Shilluk 1.7%; Lotuko 1.5%; others 9.5%

Religious affiliations Sunni Muslim 70.0%; traditional beliefs 25.0%; Christian 5.0%
Currency 1 pound (LSd) = 100 piastres
Economy Gross national product (per capita 1991) US $450
Life expectancy at birth male 53.4 yr; female 55.2 yr
Major resources petroleum, copper, iron ore, silver, other minerals, cotton, sesame
Major international organizations GATT, IBRD, IMF, NAM, OAU, UN, UNHCR, WHO

Civil war erupted in 1983 between the Muslim north and African south of Sudan, Africa's largest country, combining with drought to undermine the agricultural economy. The leading political party and the military are imposing Islamicized education and culture.

197

SURINAME

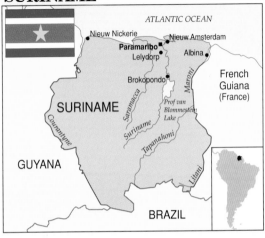

Land area 163,820 sq km (63,251 sq mi)
Major physical feature highest point:
Juliana Top 1,230 m (4,035 ft)
Population (1994) 423,000
Form of government multiparty republic
with one legislative house
Capital city Paramaribo (200,000)
Official language Dutch
Ethnic composition Asian Indian 37.0%;
Surinamese Creole 31.3%; Javanese 14.2%;
Bush Negro 8.5%; Amerindian 3.1%; Chinese
2.8%; Dutch 1.4%; other 1.7%

Religious affiliations Hindu 27.4%; Roman
Catholic 22.8%; Muslim 19.6%; Protestant
18.8%; others 11.4%
Currency 1 guilder (Sf.) = 100 cents
Economy Gross national product (per capita
1991) US $3,610
Life expectancy at birth male 67.1 yr;
female 72.1 yr
Major resources timber, fish, minerals
Major international organizations CARI-
COM, GATT, IBRD, NAM, UN, UNESCO, WHO

The former Dutch colony of Suriname lies on the north coast of South America. It was
traded by the British to the Dutch in 1667 for New Amsterdam in North America, which
became New York. Since 1980, military rule and withholding of Dutch aid have under-
mined the economy, particularly bauxite mining (the most important export industry).
Inflation and unemployment are high; there is a large black market. Amerindians and
blacks are the poorest ethnic groups. Many of them live in the undeveloped rainforested
interior, over which they are beginning to demand more control and ecological protection. Literacy is high, but most university graduates emigrate to the Netherlands.

SWAZILAND

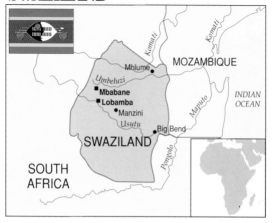

Land area 17,364 sq km (6,704 sq mi)
Major physical feature highest point: Emlembe 1,862 m (6,109 ft)
Population (1994) 936,000
Form of government monarchy with two legislative houses
Capital cities Mbabane (administrative – 38,290); Lobamba (legislative – 4,076)
Official languages Siswati (Swazi), English
Ethnic composition Swazi 84.3%; Zulu 9.9%; Tsonga 2.5%; Indian 1.6%; others 1.7%
Religious affiliations Protestant 37.3%; African Christian 28.9%; traditional beliefs 20.9%; Roman Catholic 10.8%; others 2.1%
Currency 1 lilangeni = 100 cents
Economy Gross national product (per capita 1991) US $1,060; Gross domestic product (1993) US $960 million
Life expectancy at birth male 52.4 yr; female 60.5 yr
Major resources sugar cane, cotton, coal, tobacco, asbestos, wood pulp, wildlife
Major international organizations AfBD, GATT, IBRD, NAM, OAU, UN, UNESCO, WHO

The southern African kingdom of Swaziland was under British protection 1903–68, before it achieved independence. The state borders Mozambique to the east, but otherwise is almost enclosed by South Africa, its dominant neighbor and trading partner. Political changes in the region are putting the country's conservative monarchy under pressure to introduce reform in line with South Africa's new regime. Most of the economy remains based on subsistence agriculture, and the importance of mining has declined, but manufacturing is growing substantially. The lack of diverse ethnic groups makes the country stable. Tourists are attracted by the game reserves, the spectacular mountain scenery, and the casinos; 70 percent of tourists are South Africans.

SWEDEN

Land area   449,964 sq km (173,732 sq mi)
Major physical features   highest point: Kebnekaise 2,111 m (6,926 ft); longest river: Göta-Klar 720 km (477 mi)
Population   (1994) 8,778,000
Form of government   constitutional monarchy
Capital city   Stockholm (1,503,000)
Ethnic composition   Swedish 90.8%; Finnish 3.1%; others 6.1%
Religious affiliations   Lutheran 88.9%; Roman Catholic 1.5%; Pentecostal 1.2%; others 8.4%
Currency   1 Swedish krona (SKr) = 100 öre
Economy   Gross national product (per capita 1993) US $24,740; Gross domestic product (1993) US $166,745 million
Life expectancy at birth   male 75.5 yr; female 81.2 yr
Major resources   minerals, hydropower
Major international organizations   EU, GATT, IMF, NAM, UN, UNCTAD, UNESCO, WHO

Sweden occupies the southeastern part of the Scandinavian peninsula. It has a highly developed welfare system, and one of the largest average incomes in the world.

SWITZERLAND

Land area 41,293 sq km (15,943 sq mi)
Major physical features highest point:
Monte Rosa 4,634 m (15,203 ft); longest
rivers: Rhine (part) 1,320 km (820 mi)
Population (1994) 7,040,000
Form of government federal republic
Largest cities Zurich (840,000); Geneva
(393,000); Basel (359,000); Bern (capital –
299,000); Lausanne (268,000)
Official languages German, French, Italian
Ethnic composition Swiss German 65.0%;
Swiss French 18.4%; Swiss Italian 9.8%;
Romansch 0.8%; others 6.0%

Religious affiliations Roman Catholic 47.6%;
Protestant 44.3%; Jewish 0.3%; others 7.8%
Currency 1 Swiss franc (SwF) = 100 centimes
Economy Gross national product (per capita
1993) US $35,760; Gross domestic product
(1993) US $232,161 million
Life expectancy at birth male 74.8 yr;
female 81.7 yr
Major resources timber, salt, tourism, man-
ufacturing, banking, hydroelectricity potential
Major international organizations EFTA,
GATT, IBRD, IMF, NAM, OECD, WHO

Switzerland lies at the heart of western Europe. It is an extremely stable and wealthy
nation that has built its prosperity on financial services. Today it has the world's largest
per capita income and highest standard of living. As long as it remains outside the
European Union it will remain an international tax haven, but its prominence in banking may decline with competition, and high taxes for non-residents discourage investment. The economy slowed in 1990–93 but unemployment remains at only 5 percent.

SYRIA

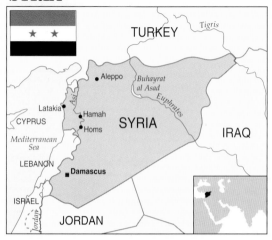

Land area 185,180 sq km (71,498 sq mi)
Major physical features highest point: Mount Hermon 2,814 m (9,232 ft); longest river: Euphrates (part) 2,720 km (1,700 mi)
Population (1994) 14,887,000
Form of government multiparty republic with one legislative house
Largest cities Damascus (capital – 1,378,000); Aleppo (1,355,000); Homs (464,000); Latakia (258,000)
Official language Arabic
Ethnic composition Arab 88.8%; Kurdish 6.3%; others 4.9%

Religious affiliations Muslim 89.6%; Christian 8.9%; others 1.5%
Currency 1 Syrian pound (S£) = 100 piastres
Economy Gross national product (per capita 1993) US $1,110
Life expectancy at birth male 65.4 yr; female 67.6 yr
Major resources petroleum, phosphates, iron ore, marble, gypsum, chrome and manganese, cotton, agriculture
Major international organizations IBRD, IDB, IMF, LORCS, NAM, OAPEC, UN, UNESCO, WHO

The Middle Eastern state of Syria (created from a former French colony in 1945) is controlled by the Ba'athist party under President Hafez Assad, but its foreign relations are precarious. After four wars with Israel, Syria is trying to obtain the return of the occupied Golan Heights on their joint border. A windfall of $3 billion in aid followed Syria's joining the coalition against Iraq in the 1991 Gulf War. This has been used for military as well as civilian projects; the defense budget takes up more than half of Syria's income. State enterprises hold back economic development, and inflation continues to be high.

TAIWAN

Land area 36,000 sq km (13,900 sq mi)
Major physical feature highest point: Yu Shan 3,997 m (13,113 ft)
Population (1994) 21,000,000
Form of government multiparty republic with two legislative houses
Largest cities T'aipei (capital – 2,718,000); Kaohsiung (1,396,000); T'aichung (774,000)
Official language Mandarin Chinese
Ethnic composition Taiwanese 84.0%; mainland Chinese 14.0%; aboriginal 2.0%

Religious affiliations folk religion 48.5%; Buddhist 43%; Christian 7.4%; others 1.1%
Currency 1 new Taiwan dollar (NT$) = 100 cents
Economy Gross national product (per capita 1991) US $8,000
Life expectancy at birth male 72.0 yr; female 78.0 yr
Major resources coal, gold, copper, petroleum, natural gas, shipbuilding, manufacturing
Major international organizations none – Taiwan is diplomatically isolated

Taiwan (formerly Formosa) lies 129 km (80 mi) off the southeast coast of China. After the Republic of China was proclaimed in Beijing in 1911, the Chinese Nationalist (KMT) party, which was losing the civil war against the Communists, fled to Taiwan in 1949. Today it is still in power, and continues to claim to be the legitimate ruler of China; communist China regards Taiwan as a province. When the United States resumed relations with mainland China in 1972, it could no longer recognize Taiwan, and the country became diplomatically isolated. The Chinese and Taiwanese governments agree that they should eventually be reunited, but Taiwan maintains the world's fifth-largest army in case of invasion. Its small, entrepreneurial economy is one of the most dynamic in the world. Shipbuilding, electronics and textiles are the most important industries.

TAJIKSTAN

Land area   143,100 sq km (55,300 sq mi)
Major physical features   highest point: Communism Peak 7,495 m (24,590 ft); longest river: Vakhsh 800 km (497 mi)
Population   (1994) 5,995,000
Form of government   multiparty republic with one legislative house
Largest cities   Dushanbe (capital – 582,000); Khudzhand = Leninabad (165,000)
Official language   Tajik
Ethnic composition   Tajik 64.9%; Uzbek 25.0%; Russian 3.5%; others 6.6%

Religious affiliations   Sunni Muslim 80%; Shi'ite Muslim 5%; other 15%
Currency   1 ruble (R) = 100 kopecks
Economy   Gross national product (per capita 1993) US $470; Gross domestic product (1993) US $2,520 million
Life expectancy at birth   male 65.9 yr; female 71.8 yr
Major resources   uranium, other minerals, hydroelectric potential, carpet making,
Major international organizations   CIS, ESCAP, IBRD, IMF, UN, UNESCO, WHO

Tajikistan, part of the Commonwealth of Independent States (CIS), was the poorest of the former Soviet republics. Following the breakup of the Soviet Union the predominantly agricultural economy collapsed and civil war broke out between the Communist government and Islamic rebels backed by supporters in Afghanistan. Only 40 percent of the workforce has formal employment. Population growth is high.

TANZANIA

Land area 885,987 sq km (342,081 sq mi)
Major physical features highest point: Kilimanjaro 5,895 m (19,340 ft); largest lake: Victoria (part) 62,940 sq km (24,300 sq mi)
Population (1994) 27,986,000
Form of government one-party republic
Capital city Dodoma (204,000)
Official languages Swahili, English
Ethnic composition African 99% (including Nyamwezi/Sukuma 21.1%; Swahili 8.8%; Hehet/Bena 6.9%; Makonde 5.9%; Haya 5.9%; other (African, European, Asian) 1%
Religious affiliations Christian 45.0%;
Muslim 35.0%; traditional beliefs and others 20.0% (Zanzibar is 99% Muslim)
Currency 1 shilling (TSh) = 100 cents
Economy Gross national product (per capita 1993) US $90; Gross domestic product (1991) US $3,079 million
Life expectancy at birth male 41.5 yr; female 45.0 yr
Major resources coffee, tea, cotton, spices, gold, diamonds, tin, phosphates, natural gas, nickel, hydropower potential, wildlife, tourism
Major international organizations GATT, IBRD, IMF, LORCS, NAM, UN, UNHCR, WHO

Tanzania, in southeast Africa, was formed by the union of Tanganyika and Zanzibar in 1964. It is one of the poorest countries in the world, but economic reform since 1986 is improving agricultural output and attracting substantial aid.

THAILAND

Land area 513,115 sq km (198,115 sq mi)
Major physical features highest point: Doi Inthanon 2,595 m (8,514 ft); longest river Mekong (part) 4,180 km (2,600 mi)
Population (1994) 59,510,000
Form of government constitutional monarchy
Largest cities Bangkok (capital – 5,876,000); Songkhla (243,000); Chiang Mai (167,000)
Official language Thai
Ethnic composition Thai 75.0%; Chinese 14.0%; others 11.0%
Religious affiliations Buddhist 94.4%;

Muslim 4.0%; Christian 0.5%; others 1.1%
Currency 1 baht (B) = 100 satang
Economy Gross national product (per capita 1993) US $2,110; Gross domestic product (1993) US $124,862 million
Life expectancy at birth male 65.0 yr; female 71.9 yr
Major resources rubber, rice, tungsten, natural gas, fish, tin, timber, tourism
Major international organizations APEC, ASEAN, ESCAP, GATT, IBRD, IMF, LORCS, NAM, UN, UNCTAD, UNESCO, UNHCR, WHO

Thailand, which lies between the Indian and Pacific oceans in southeast Asia, has one of the fastest-growing economies in the region. However, it is beginning to face competition in the manufacturing sector from cheaper labor in Vietnam and China, while its workforce is not skilled enough to compete with high-tech Japan or Taiwan.

TOGO

Land area 56,785 sq km (21,925 sq mi)
Major physical features highest point: Pic Baumann 986 m (3,235 ft); longest river: Mono 400 km (250 mi)
Population (1994) 4,255,000
Form of government one-party republic
Capital city Lomé (500,000)
Official language French, Kabre and Ewe
Ethnic composition Ewe-Adja 43.1%; Tem-Kabre 26.7%; Gurma 16.1%; Kebu-Akposo 3.8%; Yoruba 3.2%; others 7.1%
Religious affiliations traditional beliefs 58.8%; Roman Catholic 21.5%; Muslim 12.1%; Protestant 6.8%
Currency 1 CFA franc (CFAF) = 100 centimes
Economy Gross national product (per capita 1993) US $340; Gross domestic product (1993) US $1,249 million
Life expectancy at birth male 54.9 yr; female 59.1 yr
Major resources phosphates, marble, limestone, coffee, cocoa, cotton
Major international organizations GATT, IBRD, IMF, NAM, OAU, UN, WHO

Togo is a thin wedge on the map of central west Africa, between Ghana and Benin. It has a tiny strip of coast along the Gulf of Guinea. A central forest divides north from south, which are in conflict: the north controls the military and holds political power, but on average southerners are wealthier and better educated. Since 1990, a democratic movement has been trying to dislodge the party of General Eyadéma, which has been in power since 1967. Rioting in the capital of Lomé has discouraged the tourist trade, and foreign aid has been suspended.

TONGA

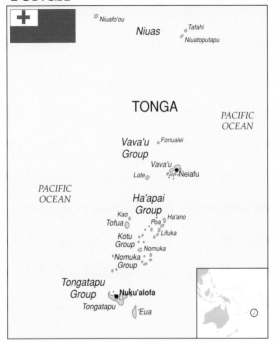

Land area 780 sq km (301 sq mi)
Major physical features largest island: Tongatapu 256 sq km (99 sq mi);
Population (1994) 105,000
Form of government constitutional monarchy
Capital city Nuku'alofa (Tongatapu, 29,000)
Official languages Tongan, English
Ethnic composition Tongan 95.5%; others 4.5%
Religious affiliations Protestant 61.3%; Roman

Catholic 16.0%; Mormon 12.1%; others 10.6%
Currency 1 pa'anga (T$ = $A) = 100 seniti
Economy Gross national product (per capita 1991) US $1,100
Life expectancy at birth male 65.6 yr; female 70.4 yr
Major resources vanilla, coconuts, bananas
Major international organizations GATT, IMF, LORCS, NAM, WHO

The kingdom of Tonga is an archipelago of 170 islands. The economy depends on tourism, cash crops and foreign aid.

TRINIDAD & TOBAGO

Land area 5,128 sq km (1,980 sq mi)
Major physical feature highest point: Mount Aripo 940 m (3,084 ft)
Population (1994) 1,328,000
Form of government multiparty republic with two legislative houses
Capital city Port-of-Spain (58,000)
Official language English
Ethnic composition black 43.0%; Asian Indian 40.0%; mixed 14.0%; others 3.0%
Religious affiliations Roman Catholic 32.2%; Protestant 27.6%; Hindu 24.3%; Muslim 5.9%; others 10.0%
Currency 1 dollar (TT$) = 100 cents
Economy Gross national product (per capita 1993) US $4,487; Gross domestic product (1993) US $3,830 million
Life expectancy at birth male 68.0 yr; female 73.0 yr
Major resources petroleum, natural gas, sugar, cocoa, coffee, citrus fruits, tourism
Major international organizations CARICOM, ECLAC, GATT, IBRD, IMF, LAES, LORCS, NAM, UN, UNCTAD, UNESCO, WHO

The Caribbean island republic of Trinidad and Tobago is made up of the two most southerly of the Caribbean Windward Islands which lie about 5 km (9 mi) off the coast of Venezuela. They gained joint independence from Britain in 1962, and since then petroleum has made the islands prosperous, accounting for about 70 percent of income. Production and revenues dropped in the 1980s, causing the economy to shrink and unemployment to rise. After a slow start, the authorities began to develop tourism, mostly on Tobago, as another source of income. Today Trinidad and Tobago are seeking closer economic ties with Colombia, Venezuela and Mexico. There is some tension between the black and Asian communities and a relatively high level of crime.

TUNISIA

Land area 154,530 sq km (59,664 sq mi)
Major physical features highest point:
Chambi 1,544 m (5,066 ft); lowest point:
Chott El Jerid – 23 m (–75 ft)
Population (1994) 8,727,000
Form of government multiparty republic
with one legislative house
Largest cities Tunis (capital – 1,395,000);
Sfax (232,000)
Official language Arabic
Ethnic composition Arab 98.2%; Berber
1.2%; French 0.2%; Italian 0.1%; others 0.3%
Official religion Islam

Religious affiliations Sunni Muslim 99.4%;
Christian 0.3%; Jewish 0.1%; others 0.2%
Currency 1 dinar (D) = 1,000 millimes
Economy Gross national product (per capita
1993) US $1,720; Gross domestic product
(1993) US $12,784 million
Life expectancy at birth male 70.8 yr;
female 75.0 yr
Major resources petroleum, phosphates,
iron ore, lead, zinc, salt, tourism, agriculture
Major international organizations AfDB,
GATT, IBRD, IDB, IMF, LORCS, NAM, OAPEC,
OAS, OAU, UN, UNCTAD, WHO

Tunisia, in North Africa, is one of the most liberal of the Arab states, attracting two million tourists every year. The diverse economy grew rapidly in the mid 1980s, but low oil prices, drought, a foreign-exchange crisis and the Gulf War of 1991 caused a downturn in its fortunes. The rise of Islamic fundamentalism is also posing new political problems.

TURKEY

Land area   779,452 sq km (300,948 sq mi)
Major physical features   highest point:
Ararat 5,165 m (16,945 ft); longest river: Kizil
Irmak 1,150 km (715 mi)
Population   (1994) 62,154,000
Form of government   multiparty republic
with one legislative house
Largest cities   Istanbul (6,407,000); Ankara
(capital – 3,022,000); Izmir (2,665,000)
Official language   Turkish
Ethnic composition   Turkish 80%; Kurdish 20%
Religious affiliations   Sunni Muslim 99.2%;

Eastern Orthodox 0.3%; others 0.5%
Currency   1 Turkish lira (TL) = 100 kurus
Economy   Gross national product (per capita
1993) US $2,970; Gross domestic product
(1993) US $156,413 million
Life expectancy at birth   male 68.6 yr;
female 73.4 yr
Major resources   minerals, agriculture,
tourism, manufacturing
Major international organizations   GATT,
IBRD, IMF, LORCS, NATO, OECD, UN, UNC-
TAD, UNESCO, UNHCR, WHO

Bridging Europe and Asia, and occupying a strategic position at the entrance to the
Black Sea, the Middle Eastern nation of Turkey has strong links to both cultures. Rapid
economic growth in the 1980s gave way to a slump in the 1990s as inflation, public debt
and interest rates rose dramatically. A number of banks have failed, and the stock
exchange has dropped by almost 50 percent. Tourism, a valuable industry, is under
threat from sporadic violence caused by the rebel Kurdistan Workers' Party; economic
activity in the southeast has been badly disrupted. Turkey is seeking emergency aid to
stabilize the economy and to allow the country to return to the foreign capital markets.

TURKMENISTAN

Land area 488,100 sq km (188,500 sq mi)
Major physical features highest point:
Firyuza 2,942 m (9,652 ft); longest river: Amu
Darya (part) 2,539 km (1,578 mi)
Population (1994) 3,995,000
Form of government multiparty republic
with two legislative houses
Capital city Ashkhabad (407,000)
Official language Turkmenian
Ethnic composition Turkmen 73.3%; Russian
9.8%; Uzbek 9.0%; Kazakh 2.0%; others 5.9%
Religious affiliations Sunni Muslim 87.0%;

Eastern Orthodox 11.0%; others 2.0%
Currency manat (since November 1993)
Economy Gross national product (per capita
1993) US $1,650; Gross domestic product
(1993) US $5,156 million
Life expectancy at birth male 61.6 yr;
female 68.8 yr
Major resources petroleum, natural gas,
coal, sulfur, salt, cotton, textiles, carpets
Major international organizations CIS,
EBRD, ESCAP, IBRD, IDB, IMF, UN, UNCTAD,
UNESCO, WHO

Since independence, the former Soviet republic of Turkmenistan has successfully
exploited its two major resources, natural gas and cotton, to earn foreign revenue that
has stabilized the economy throughout a period of political reorganization. Free-market
reforms are being approached cautiously, and Turkmenistan still trades principally with
its CIS neighbors. The terrain is mostly desert, inhabited by nomadic cattle-herding
people. Social conflict tends to be tribal rather than ethnic.

TUVALU

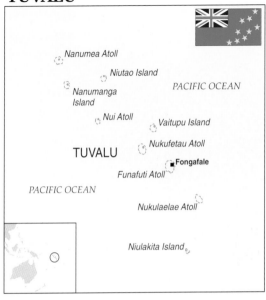

Land area 24 sq km (9 sq mi)
Major physical feature largest island: Vaitupu 5 sq km (2 sq mi)
Population (1994) 10,000
Form of government constitutional monarchy
Capital city Fongafale (Funafuti, 3,000)
Official languages Tuvaluan, English
Ethnic composition Tuvaluan (Polynesian) 91.2%; mixed 7.2%; others 1.6%
Religious affiliations Church of Tuvalu (Congregational) 96.9%; Seventh-Day Adventist 1.4%; Baha'i 1.0%; others 0.7%
Currency 1 Tuvaluan dollar ($T) = 100 cents
Economy Gross national product (per capita 1991) US $700
Life expectancy at birth male 61.6 yr; female 64.1 yr
Major resources fish, copra
Major international organizations ESCAP, UNESCO, WHO

The nine coral atolls of the South Pacific republic of Tuvalu, 3,000 km (1,864 mi) east of Papua New Guinea, have poor soil and no fresh water. They are too remote to support tourism, and lack mineral resources. The population depends on subsistence farming and fishing. Some of Tuvalu's vast maritime zone is rented out for fees. Australia, New Zealand and the UK set up a trust in 1987 which provides an annual income.

UGANDA

Land area 197,040 sq km (76,080 sq mi)
Major physical features highest point: Mount Stanley 5,110 m (16,765 ft); largest lake: Lake Victoria (part) 62,940 sq km (24,300 sq mi)
Population (1994) 19,122,000
Form of government republic with interim military government
Capital city Kampala (773,000)
Official languages English, Swahili
Ethnic composition Gandan 17.8%; Teso 8.9%; Nkole 8.2%; Soga 8.2%; Gisu 7.2%; Chiga 6.8%; Lango 6.0%; Rwandan 5.8%; Acholi 4.6%; others 26.5%

Religious affiliations Roman Catholic 33.0%; Protestant 33.0%; Muslim 16.0%; others 18.0%
Currency 1 shilling (USh) = 100 cents
Economy Gross national product (per capita 1993) US $180; Gross domestic product (1993) US $3,037 million
Life expectancy at birth male 49.4 yr; female 52.7 yr
Major resources copper, cobalt, limestone, coffee, cotton, tea
Major international organizations AfDB, GATT, IBRD, IMF, LORCS, NAM, OAU, UN, UNCTAD, UNESCO, UNHCR, WHO

One of the poorest countries in the world, landlocked Uganda in central east Africa, is rebuilding itself after 26 years of civil war. It is just beginning to exploit its natural resources, but in the meantime coffee is the main export crop, and most people live by subsistence agriculture. Inflation is declining from a peak of 300% in 1987, and the country's infrastructure is being rebuilt. Literacy and standards of living are still low, but Uganda's human rights record has improved dramatically in recent years.

UKRAINE

Land area 603,700 sq km (233,100 sq mi)
Major physical features highest point: Hoverla 2,061 m (6,762 ft); longest river: Dnieper (part) 2,280 km (1,420 mi)
Population (1994) 51,847,000
Form of government multiparty republic
Largest cities Kiev (capital – 2,616,000); Kharkov (1,618,000)
Official language Ukrainian
Ethnic composition Ukrainian 73.0%; Russian 22.0%; others 5.0%
Religious affiliations Eastern Catholic, Eastern Orthodox, Roman Catholic and Jewish
Currency Grivna (since 1994)
Economy Gross national product (per capita 1993) US $2,210; Gross domestic product (1993) US $109,078 million
Life expectancy at birth male 65.4 yr; female 74.8 yr
Major resources iron ore, coal, natural gas, oil, timber, mercury, nickel, grain, meat
Major international organizations CIS, IBRD, IMF, UN, UNCTAD, UNESCO, WHO

Since the 16th century Ukraine has been occupied by Russia, Poland and Turkey; Russia wielded political control from the 18th century until Ukraine regained full independence following the break-up of the Soviet Union in August 1991. Today Ukraine is the second most populous republic in the CIS, and ranks second in its abundance of economic resources . The world's worst civil nuclear disaster occurred at Chernobyl in 1986.

UNITED ARAB EMIRATES

Land area 77,700 sq km (30,000 sq mi)

Major physical feature highest point: Jabal Hafib 1,189 m (3,901 ft)

Population (1994) 2,791,000

Form of government federal monarchy with one appointed council

Largest cities Dubai (266,000); Abu Dhabi (capital – 243,000); Sharjah (125,000)

Official language Arabic

Ethnic composition Emirian 20%; other Arab 22%; South Asian 50%; others 8%

Official religion Islam

Religious affiliations Sunni Muslim 80.0%; Shi'ite Muslim 16.0%; Christian 3.8%; other 0.2%

Currency 1 UAE dirham (Dh) = 100 fils

Economy Gross national product (per capita 1993) US $21,430; Gross domestic product (1993) US $34,935 million

Life expectancy at birth male 70.1 yr; female 74.4 yr

Major resources petroleum, natural gas

Major international organizations GATT, IBRD, IDB, IMF, LORCS, NAM, OAPEC, OPEC, UN, UNCTAD, UNESCO, WHO

The United Arab Emirates, on the edge of the Persian Gulf, is an oil-rich state. In the 1990s oil and gas exports account for 40 percent of GDP, and have transformed the UAE from an impoverished region of desert principalities to a wealthy nation. Like others in the region, the UAE has large numbers of foreign workers, skilled and unskilled. It is politically moderate; Western expatriates live without restrictions, and women have equal rights under the law. To maintain economic strength, the government is promoting privatization and entrepreneurship. Education and healthcare are free to citizens.

UNITED KINGDOM

The United Kingdom lies off the Atlantic coast of mainland Europe, and consists of England, Scotland and Wales (Great Britain) and Northern Ireland. The English, Irish, Scottish and Welsh are all centuries-old mixes of the tribes that inhabited and conquered the territory. Since 1945 the United Kingdom has also become home to thousands of immigrants from commonwealth countries, notably the West Indies, Pakistan and India, which have transformed Britain into a multicultural society. In the 19th century Britain was an industrial giant with a vast empire; the destruction of two world wars and the break-up of the empire have caused a dramatic change in fortune. With most mineral sources depleted, the economy has shifted to rely on services and tourism, and to focus much of its trade within the European Community. The discovery of natural gas and North Sea Oil off the coast of Scotland has been an economic mainstay.

Land area 244,110 sq km (94,251 sq mi)
Major physical features highest point: Ben Nevis 1,344 m (4,408 ft); longest river: Thames 340 km (210 mi)
Population (1994) 58,135,000
Form of government multiparty constitutional monarchy with two legislative houses
Largest cities London (capital – 6,378,000); Manchester (1,669,000); Birmingham (1,400,000); Liverpool (1,060,000); Glasgow (730,000)
Official language English
Ethnic composition White (English, Scottish, Welsh, Irish) 91.9%; Black Caribbean 0.9%; Black African 0.4%; Indian 1.5%; Pakistani 0.8%; Bangladeshi 0.3%; Chinese 0.3%; other Asian 0.3%; others 3.6%

Religious affiliations Anglican 56.8%; Roman Catholic 13.1%; nonreligious 8.8%; Scottish Presbyterian 7.0%; Methodist 4.3%; other Christians 5.7%; Muslim 1.4%; Jewish 0.8%; Hindu 0.7%; Sikh 0.4%; others 1.0%
Currency 1 pound sterling (£) = 100 new pence
Economy Gross national product (per capita 1993) US $18,060; Gross domestic product (1993) US $819,038 million
Life expectancy at birth male 73.9 yr; female 79.7 yr
Major resources natural gas, tourism, banking and financial services, coal, petroleum
Major international organizations ESCAP, EU, G-7, GATT, EBRD, IBRD, IMF, INTERPOL, LORCS, NATO, OECD, UN, UNTAD, UNHCR, UNPROFOR, WHO

Countries of the Union
(with population for 1991)

England	(46,382,050)	Scotland	(4,962,152)
Wales	(2,811,865)	Northern Ireland	(1,573,282)

Territories and Dependencies
(with population for 1993)

Anguilla	(7,000)	Gibraltar	(32,000)
Ascension	(1,500)	Hong Kong	(5,900,000)
Bahamas	(270,000)	Isle of Man	(123,300)
Bermuda	(61,000)	Montserrat	(13,000)
British Indian Ocean Territory (no permanent population)		Pitcairn Islands	(60)
		St. Helena	(8,000)
British Virgin Islands	(13,000)	South Georgia & the South Sandwich Islands (no permanent population)	
Cayman Islands	(30,000)		
Channel Islands	(20,600)		
Falkland Islands	(2,000)	Turks and Caicos Islands	(11,000)

Shetland
Islands

Orkney
Islands

Outer
Hebrides

SCOTLAND

NORTHERN
IRELAND

Isle of
Man

UNITED KINGDOM

ENGLAND

WALES

London

UNITED STATES

The United States is the fourth largest country in land area (after Russia, Canada, and China) and third largest in population (after China and India). However, since 1945 when it swapped isolationism for political involvement, it has become the world's leading nation in political and cultural influence. It also has the largest gross domestic product among major industrial nations. It owes this success to its plentiful natural resources, a rich cultural mix, and a strong sense of national identity. The first settlers probably crossed from Siberia and Alaska between 30,000 and 10,000 years ago, and their descendants, the Native Americans developed a wide variety of cultural settlements across the country. The earliest European settlers were the Spanish and Portuguese who arrived in the 15th century, followed closely by the Dutch and English who established a colony which survived until American Independence in 1776. Since then waves of emigration have made the U.S. the cultural melting pot of the world.

Land area 9,166,600 sq km (3,539,242.5 sq mi)

Major physical features highest point: Mount McKinley 6,194 m (20,320 ft); longest river: Mississippi–Missouri 6,020 km (3,740 mi); largest lake: Lake Superior (part) 83,270 sq km (32,150 sq mi)

Population (1994) 260,713,000

Form of government federal multiparty republic with two legislative houses

Large cities/metropolitan areas (population in millions, 1992. The second number gives the population of the metropolitan area of which the city is part) New York (7.312/19.67); Los Angeles (3.49/15.048); Chicago (2.768/8.41); Houston (1.69/3.962); Philadelphia (1.553/5.939); San Diego (1.149/2.601); Dallas (1.022/4.215); Phoenix (1.012/2.33); Detroit (1.012/5.24); San Francisco (0.729/6.41); Washington DC (capital – 0.585/6.92); Boston (0.552/5.439)

Official language English

Ethnic composition White 83.4%; Black 12.4%; Asian 3.3%; Native American 0.8%

Religious affiliations Protestant 56%; Roman Catholic 28%; Jewish 2%; others 4%; nonreligious 10%

Currency 1 United States dollar = 100 cents

Economy Gross national product (per capita 1993) US $24,740; Gross domestic product (1993) US $6,259,899 million

Life expectancy at birth male 72.6 yr; female 79.4 yr

Major resources coal, petroleum, natural gas, timber, copper, lead, molybdenum, phosphates, uranium, bauxite, gold, iron, mercury, nickel, potash, silver, tungsten, zinc

Major international organizations AfDB, APEC, EBRD, ESCAP, G-7, GATT, IBRD, IMF, INTERPOL, LORCS, NATO, OECD, UN, UNESCO, UNHCR, UNIDO, WHO

Dependencies and Overseas Territories

(with population for 1993)

American Samoa (53,000)

Baker Island (no permanent population)

Guam (145,000)

Howland Island (no permanent population)

Jarvis Island (no permanent population)

Johnston Atoll (327)*

Kingman Reef (no permanent population)

Midway Islands (453)*

Navassa Island (no permanent population)

Northern Mariana Islands (23,000)

Palmyra Atoll (no permanent population)

Puerto Rico (3,600,000)

U.S. Virgin Islands (118,000)

Wake Island (302)*

* 1991 figures

CONN.	CONNECTICUT
D.C.	DISTRICT OF COLUMBIA
DEL.	DELAWARE
MD.	MARYLAND
MASS.	MASSACHUSETTS
MISS.	MISSISSIPPI
N.H.	NEW HAMPSHIRE
N.J.	NEW JERSEY
R.I.	RHODE ISLAND
VE.	VERMONT
W.V.	WEST VIRGINIA

States of the Union (with population for 1993)

Alabama	(4,187,000)	Nebraska	(1,607,000)
Alaska	(599,000)	Nevada	(1,389,000)
Arizona	(3,936,000)	New Hampshire	(1,125,000)
Arkansas	(2,424,000)	New Jersey	(7,879,000)
California	(31,211,000)	New Mexico	(1,616,000)
Colorado	(3,566,000)	New York	(17,761,000)
Connecticut	(3,277,000)	North Carolina	(6,945,000)
Delaware	(700,000)	North Dakota	(635,000)
Florida	(13,679,000)	Ohio	(11,091,000)
Georgia	(6,917,000)	Oregon	(3,032,000)
Hawaii	(1,172,000)	Oklahoma	(3,231,000)
Idaho	(1,099,000)	Pennsylvania	(12,048,000)
Illinois	(11,697,000)	Rhode Island	(996,000)
Indiana	(5,713,000)	South Carolina	(3,643,000)
Iowa	(2,814,000)	South Dakota	(715,000)
Kansas	(2,531,000)	Tennessee	(5,099,000)
Kentucky	(3,789,000)	Texas	(18,031,000)
Louisiana	(4,295,000)	Utah	(1,860,000)
Maine	(1,239,000)	Vermont	(576,000)
Maryland	(4,965,000)	Virginia	(6,491,000)
Massachusetts	(6,012,000)	Washington	(5,255,000)
Michigan	(9,478,000)	West Virginia	(1,820,000)
Minnesota	(4,517,000)	Wisconsin	(5,038,000)
Mississippi	(2,643,000)	Wyoming	(470,000)
Missouri	(5,234,000)		
Montana	(839,000)	District of Columbia	(578,000)

URUGUAY

Land area 175,016 sq km (67,574 sq mi)
Major physical feature highest point: Cerro de las Ánimas 501 m (1,643 ft)
Population (1994) 3,199,000
Form of government multiparty republic with two legislative houses
Largest cities Montevideo (capital – 1,248,000); Salto (71,880); Paysandú (62,412)
Official language Spanish
Ethnic composition Spanish/Italian 88.5%; mestizo 3.0%; mulatto 1.2%; others 7.3%
Religious affiliations Roman Catholic 59.5%; nonreligious 35.1%; others 5.4%
Currency the peso
Economy Gross national product (per capita 1993) US $3,830; Gross domestic product (1993) US $13,144 million
Life expectancy at birth male 70.9 yr; female 77.5 yr
Major resources agate, amethyst, gold, livestock, wool, rice, hydropower, tourism
Major international organizations GATT, IBRD, IMF, LAES, LAIA, LORCS, NAM, UN, UNCTAD, UNESCO, WHO

Uruguay, the smallest country in South America, is on the southeast coast between Brazil and Argentina. Colonized by the Spanish and Portuguese from the 15th century, Uruguay became independent in 1828. A military coup in 1973 led to 12 years of dictatorship, and nearly half a million Uruguayans emigrated; most have since returned. The government is now reconstructing the economy and modernizing the country's infrastructure . The livestock industry plays an important role in the economy. Sheep and beef cattle are reared for their meat, hides, wool and other byproducts. The food industry, textiles, chemicals, and tourism also make important contributions to the economy.

UZBEKISTAN

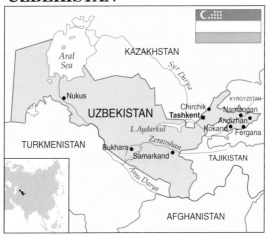

Land area 447,400 sq km (172,700 sq mi)
Major physical features highest point: Beshtor Peak 4,299 m (14,104 ft); largest lake: Aral Sea (part) 66,500 sq km (25,700 sq mi)
Population (1994) 22,609,000
Form of government multiparty republic with one legislative house
Largest cities Tashkent (capital – 2,094,000); Samarkand (370,000); Bukhara (228,000)
Official language Uzbek
Ethnic composition Uzbek 71.4%; Russian 8.3%; Tatar 2.4%; Kazakh 4.1%; Tajik 4.7%; others 9.1%
Religious affiliations Sunni Muslim 88.0%;

Eastern Orthodox 10.0%; other 2%
Currency the som (since 1994)
Economy Gross national product (per capita 1993) US $970; Gross domestic product (1993) US $20,425 million
Life expectancy at birth male 65.3 yr; female 72.0 yr
Major resources natural gas, petroleum, coal, uranium, gold, silver, copper, lead, zinc, tungsten, molybdenum, cotton, textiles, grain, fruits and vegetables, livestock
Major international organizations CIS, ESCAP, IBRD, IMF, NAM, UN, UNCTAD, WHO

The small, landlocked Central Asian republic of Uzbekistan became independent with the break-up of the Soviet Union in 1991. Although it is one of the poorest states in the region, with a large rural population crowded onto a small amount of arable land, it has significant mineral resources and fossil fuels, and grows a range of cash crops. Economic reform was resisted until 1993, when inflation rose sharply; since then market reforms have been required by leading international financial organizations. Ethnic tension is being firmly controlled by the government, which remains authoritarian.

VANUATU

Land area 14,760 sq km (5,699 sq mi)
Major physical features largest island: Espiritu Santo 3,678 sq km (1,420 sq mi); highest point: Tabwémanasana 1,879 m (6,165 ft)
Population (1994) 170,000
Form of government multiparty republic
Capital city Port-Vila (19,000)
Official languages French, English
Ethnic composition Ni-Vanuatu 97.0%; other 3.0%
Religious affiliations Presbyterian 36.7%; Anglican 15.1%; Roman Catholic 14.8%; other

Christian 14.9%; traditional beliefs 7.6%; nonreligious 10.9%
Currency 1 vatu (VT) = 100 centimes
Economy Gross national product (per capita 1993) US $1,120
Life expectancy male 57.5 yr; female 61.1 yr
Major resources fish, hardwood timber, manganese, tourism
Major international organizations ESCAP, GATT, IBRD, IMF, NAM, UN, UNCTAD, WHO

The South Pacific islands of Vanuatu, near Fiji, became independent in 1980. Most of the population lives by subsistence agriculture. Fishing and tourism are the most important industries. Anglo-French control before 1980 has left behind political divisions.

VATICAN CITY

Land area 0.44 sq km (0.17 sq mi)
Population (1994) 1,000
Form of government city-state with one appointed absolute ruler: the Pope
Armed forces Swiss Guard, 100

Official languages Italian, Latin
Official religion Roman Catholicism
Religious affiliations Roman Catholic 100%
Currency 1 Vatican lira (VL) = Italian lira (Lit) = 100 centesimi

The last remnant of the former Papal States, the Vatican City, on the west bank of the Tiber river, is enclosed by the city of Rome. The smallest independent state in the world, it is the headquarters of the Roman Catholic Church, which refused to be incorporated into the Italian nation in 1860. It is unique in that it has no actual land area, only the buildings that house the church's administration and other functions. Other buildings under Vatican control include the Pope's summer palace at Castel Gandolfo, 20 km (12.4 mi) outside Rome. The Vatican does not have an independent economy, but it has its own radio station, banking, postal and telephone systems, and strong tourist and publishing industries. The church's assets – priceless art, international real estate and gold reserves – make it one of the wealthiest institutions in the world.

VENEZUELA

Land area 912,050 sq km (352,144 sq mi)
Major physical features highest point: Pico Bolívar 5,007 m (16,427 ft); longest river: Orinoco 2,060 km (1,280 mi)
Population (1994) 20,562,000
Form of government federal multiparty republic with two legislative houses
Largest cities Caracas (capital – 3,247,000); Maracaibo (1,295,000); Valencia (1,135,000); Maracay (857,000); Barquisimeto (718,000)
Official language Spanish
Ethnic composition mestizo 69.0%; white 20.0%; black 9.0%; Amerindian 2.0%

Religious affiliations Roman Catholic 91.7%; others 8.3%
Currency 1 bolívar (B; plural Bs) = 100 centimos
Economy Gross national product (per capita 1993) US $2,840; Gross domestic product (1993) US $59,995 million
Life expectancy at birth male 70.1 yr; female 76.0 yr
Major resources petroleum, natural gas, gold, diamonds, iron ore, bauxite, livestock
Major international organizations CARICOM, GATT, IBRD, IMF, LORCS, NAM, OPEC, UN, UNCTAD, UNESCO, UNHCR, WHO

Venezuela, on the northern coast of South America, was a former Spanish colony that became independent in 1811. It has rich reserves of oil, but continuing domestic difficulties have hindered prosperity. Economic growth fluctuated in the 1990s as market reforms were introduced, and the removal of price controls led to urban riots in 1991. In recent years government has been unstable. Venezuela's previous president was impeached for corruption in 1993, and currently there are fears of a military coup.

228

VIETNAM

Land area   331,653 sq km (128,052 sq mi)
Major physical features   highest point: Fan Si Pan 3,143 m (10,312 ft); longest river: Mekong (part) 4,180 km (2,600 mi)
Population   (1994) 73,104,000
Form of government   one-party republic
Largest cities   Ho Chi Minh City (3,169,000); Hanoi (capital – 2,571,000); Haiphong (1,279,000)

Ethnic composition Vietnamese 87.3%; Tai 1.7%; Khmer 1.4%; Muong 1.3%; Nung 1.1%; others 7.2%
Religious affiliations Buddhist 55.3%; other 43.7%
Currency 1 dong (D) = 10 hao = 100 xu
Gross national product (per capita 1993) $170
Life expectancy male 63.4 yr; female 67.6 yr
Major resources offshore oil, rice, timber
Major international organizations ASEAN, IBRD, LORCS, NAM, UN, WHO

The Southeast Asian republic of Vietnam is gradually recovering from the destruction of the war with the United States (1965–75). The US economic embargo was finally lifted in 1993; Vietnam now receives substantial aid. The economy is market oriented and is expected by some to be a rising power in Asia. Rice and crude oil are the chief exports.

WESTERN SAMOA

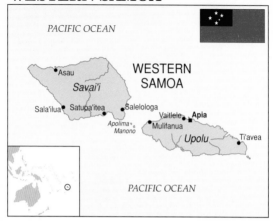

Land area 2,831 sq km (1,093 sq mi)
Major physical features largest island: Savai'i 1,707 sq km (659 sq mi); highest point: Silisili (Savai'i) 1,858 m (6,096 ft)
Population (1994) 204,000
Form of government multiparty constitutional monarchy with one legislative house
Capital city Apia (Upolu Island, 33,000)
Official languages Samoan, English
Ethnic composition Samoan (Polynesian) 92.6%; Eurasian 7.0%; European 0.4%

Religious affiliations Protestant 63.5%; Roman Catholic 21.7%; Mormon 8.3%; other 6.5%
Currency 1 tala (WS$) = 100 sene
Economy Gross national product (per capita 1991) US $930
Life expectancy at birth male 65.6 yr; female 70.5 yr
Major resources hardwood, fish, copra
Major international organizations ESCAP, IBRD, IDA, LORCS, UN, UNCTAD, UNESCO, WHO

The former German protectorate of Western Samoa, in the South Pacific, became independent in 1962 after being administered by New Zealand following World War I. Its nine islands are some of the least developed in the world, owing partly to their remote location and partly to the conservative nature of the society, which remains tribal. The economy is overwhelmingly agricultural, relying on exports of coconut oil and copra, and increasingly on income from tourism. Revenues are boosted by substantial amounts of foreign aid, mostly from Australia, Japan, New Zealand and the European Union. Unemployment is high, and the government is the major employer. Many Samoans work abroad, especially in New Zealand and American Samoa. Light manufacturing and service industries (especially offshore banking) are growing rapidly.

YEMEN

Land area   527,970 sq km (203,849 sq mi)
Major physical feature   highest point: an-Nabi Shu'ayb 3,760 m (12,336 ft)
Population   (1994) 11,105,000
Form of government   multiparty republic with one legislative house
Largest cities   San'a (capital – 427,000); Aden (264,000); Ta'izz (178,000)
Official language   Arabic
Ethnic composition   Arab 97.5%; African 1.2%; others 1.3%
Official religion   Islam

Religious affiliations   Sunni Muslim 53.0%; Shi'ite Muslim 46.9%; others 0.1%
Currency   1 Yemeni dinar = 26 Yemeni rials
Economy   Gross national product (per capita 1993) US $585; Gross domestic product (1993) US $11,958 million
Life expectancy at birth   male 50.3 yr; female 52.6 yr
Major resources   Petroleum, fish, rocksalt, marble, coal, gold, nickel, copper
Major international organizations   IBRD, IMF, NAM, UN, UNESCO, WHO

The Republic of Yemen was created in 1990 by the unification of the former Yemen Arab Republic on the Red Sea coast and the People's Democratic Republic of Yemen which overlooked the Gulf of Aden. Yemen is a desert country, and the discovery of petroleum is relatively recent. Subsistence farming dominates, combined with cash crops of coffee and cotton. There are few surfaced roads, no railroads, and limited communications.

YUGOSLAVIA (SERBIA/MONTENEGRO)

Land area 25,715 sq km (9,929 sq mi)

Major physical features highest point: Daravica 2,656 m (8,712 ft); longest rivers: Danube (part) 2,850 km (1,770 mi); Morava 351 km (218 mi)

Population (1994) 10,400,000

Form of government parliamentary democracy (unstable)

Armed forces information not available

Capital city Belgrade (1,470,000)

Official languages Serbo-Croat

Ethnic composition Serb 63.0%; Albanian 14.0%; Montenegrin 6.0%; Hungarian 4.0%; others 13.0%

Religious affiliations Othodox 65.0%; Muslim 19.0%; Roman Catholic 4.0%; Protestant 1.0%; others 11.0%

Currency 1 dinar (Din) = 100 paras

Economy figures not available

Life expectancy at birth not available

Major resources agriculture; mining; trade

Major international organizations none

Serbia and Montenegro comprise the rump state of Yugoslavia following the 1990 breakup of the six republics (Slovenia, Croatia, Bosnia Herzegovina, Macedonia, Serbia and Montenegro) that made up former Yugoslavia. Although rich in mineral and agricultural resources, Yugoslavia's economy has been severely damaged since 1990 by civil war and international sanctions imposed to quell Serbian territorial claims.

ZAIRE

Land area 2,345,095 sq km (905,446 sq mi)
Major physical features highest point:
Mount Stanley 5,110 m (16,765 ft); largest
lake: Lake Tanganyika (part) 32,900 sq km
(12,700 sq mi)
Population (1994) 42,684,000
Form of government one-party republic
Capital city Kinshasa (2,796,000)
Official language French
Ethnic composition Luba 18.0%; Kongo
16.1%; Mongo 13.5%; Rwanda 10.3%; Azande
6.1%; Bangi/Ngale 5.8%; Rundi 3.8%; Teke
2.7%; Boa 2.3%; Chokwe 1.8%; Lugbara 1.6%;

Banda 1.4%; others 16.6%
Religious affiliations Roman Catholic
50.0%; Protestant 20.0%; Kimbanguist 10.0%;
Muslim 10.0%; others 10.0%
Currency 1 zaïre (Z) = 100 makuta
Economy Gross national product (per capita
1991) US $220
Life expectancy at birth male 45.6 yr;
female 49.3 yr
Major resources Cobalt, copper, cadmium,
petroleum, diamonds, gold, silver, zinc
Major international organizations GATT,
IBRD, IMF, UN, UNESCO, UNHCR, WHO

Zaire straddles the equator at the very heart of the African continent, and is bordered
by nine other nations. It contains one of the world's largest tropical rainforests.

ZAMBIA

Land area 752,614 sq km (290,586 sq mi)
Major physical feature highest point: Nyika Plateau (part) 2,164 m (7,100 ft)
Population (1994) 9,188,000
Form of government multiparty republic with one legislative house
Capital city Lusaka (921,000)
Official language English
Ethnic composition Bemba 36.2%; Maravi 17.6%; Tonga 15.1%; Northwestern tribes 10.1%; Barotze 8.2%; Mambwe 4.6%; Tumbuka 4.6%; others 3.6%
Religious affiliations Christian 50–75%; Muslim and Hindu 24–49%; indigenous beliefs 1.0%
Currency 1 Zambian kwacha = 100 ngwee
Economy Gross national product (per capita 1993) US $380; Gross domestic product (1993) US $3,685 million
Life expectancy at birth male 43.8 yr; female 44.5 yr
Major resources copper, timber, cobalt, zinc, lead, coal, emeralds, gold, silver, tobacco, sugar, cotton, fisheries
Major international organizations GATT, IBRD, IMF, LORCS, NAM, UN, UNESCO, WHO

Zambia is a landlocked country in south-central Africa. Most of the terrain is a mixture of woodland and savanna grassland, but in the west there are forests of Rhodesian teak. Copper mining dominates the economy; Zambia is the world's fourth largest producer. It also has deposits of other precious metals and gemstones. Tobacco, sugar and cotton are grown as cash crops, but most agriculture is at subsistence level. Industry (textiles, chemicals, petroleum refining) is being developed. Zambia's history during the struggle for independence (achieved in 1964) has been closely linked with its neighbor, Zimbabwe.

ZIMBABWE

Land area 390,759 sq km (150,873 sq mi)

Major physical feature highest point: Inyangani 2,592 m (8,504 ft)

Population (1994) 10,700,000

Form of government one-party republic

Largest cities Harare (capital – 681,000); Bulawayo (500,000)

Official language English

Ethnic composition Shona 70.8%; Ndebele 15.8%; other Africans 11.0%; European 2.0%; Asian 0.1%; others 0.3%

Religious affiliations traditional beliefs 40.4%; Protestant 17.5%; African Christian 13.6%; Roman Catholic 11.7%; others 16.8%

Currency 1 Zimbabwe dollar= 100 cents

Economy Gross national product (per capita 1993) US $520; Gross domestic product (1993) US $4,986 million

Life expectancy at birth male 59.0 yr; female 63.0 yr

Major resources gold, asbestos, coal, metal ores, tobacco, cotton, sugar cane, tea, coffee

Major international organizations GATT, NAM, UN, UNESCO, WHO

Zimbabwe, formerly Southern Rhodesia, lies in southern Africa between the Zambezi and Limpopo rivers. After decades of political struggle the country achieved independence in 1980. It continues to grow cash crops based on the old plantation system, and is beginning to develop a strong manufacturing sector to make the most of its resources.

ANTARCTICA

Land area 14,000,000 sq km (5,405,430 sq mi), or 1.5 times the size of the U.S.
Population There are no permanent inhabitants of Antarctica, only seasonally staffed research stations
Year-round stations: 41 total
Argentina 6, Australia 3, Chile 3, China 2, Finland 1, France 1, Germany 1, India 1, Japan 2, South Korea 1, New Zealand 1, Poland 1, South Africa 3, United Kingdom 5, Uruguay 1, United States 3, Former Soviet Union 6
Summer stations: 38 (not including US)
Argentina 7, Australia 3, Chile 5, Germany 3,

India 1, Italy 1, Japan 4, New Zealand 2, Norway 1, Peru 1, South Africa 1, Spain 1, Sweden 2, United Kingdom 1, United States numerous stations, former Soviet Union 5 (the disintegration of the former Soviet Union has put the status of its facilities in doubt).
Major Resources none presently exploited, but Antarctica has small reserves of iron ore, chromium, copper, gold, nickel, platinum, coal and hydrocarbons
Economic Activity there is no economic activity based in the region, apart from offshore fishing and small-scale tourism, both run from abroad

Antarctica is a massive land area, more than 95 percent of which is covered with an ice-cap, created by thousands of years of accumulated snowfall. Ice-free coastal areas include parts of southern Victoria Land, Wilkes Land, the Antarctic Peninsula area, and parts of Ross Island on McMurdo Sound. Floating ice shelves constitute some 11 percent of the continent. It is the highest continent in the world, rising an average of over 2,000 m (7,000 ft) above sea level. It is also the driest continent, although it holds almost nine tenths of the world's ice. If Antarctica's ice cap were to melt, it would raise the world's sea level by 65m (210 ft). The long Transantarctic Mountain chain runs across the whole continent, dividing it into two unequal parts: Lesser Antarctica, mostly within western longitudes; and the massive semicircle of Greater Antarctica. Several other mountain ranges emerge around the fringes of the ice cap, and there are active volcanoes in Lesser Antarctica, notably on the islands north of the Weddell Sea.

August is the coldest month when temperatures fall to between -40°F to -95°F (-40°C to -70°C) on the inland ice sheet. These hostile conditions coupled with long months of darkness in the winter, mean that plant life is limited to mosses and lichens. There are no land mammals in the region, but whales and seals live in the icy seas, and the area is a haven for arctic birds. Emperor penguins, Antarctic petrels, and South Polar skuas breed here and nowhere else, and more than 40 species live in the area.

During the International Geophysical Year (1957–58) scientists from twelve nations spent the winter in research stations scattered across the region, studying Antarctica's unique environment. The following year, the same twelve nations signed the Antarctic Treaty reserving the continent for peaceful and non-political scientific study. The treaty also prohibits military activity of any kind in the region, including weapons testing. During the 1970s the signatories applied limits on seal trapping and whaling, activities that had almost reduced some species to extinction. In the 1980s scientists discovered massive damage to the ozone layer in the atmosphere above the South Pole.

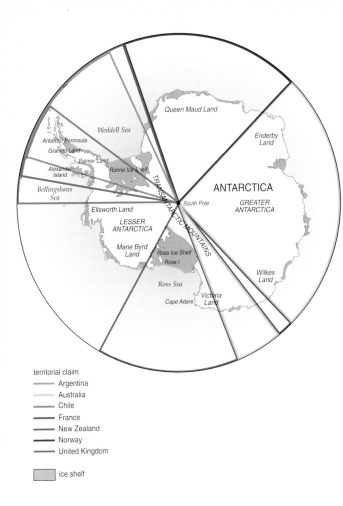

territorial claim
- Argentina
- Australia
- Chile
- France
- New Zealand
- Norway
- United Kingdom

ice shelf

THE WORLD'S TIME ZONES

| 1 a.m. | 2 a.m. | 3 a.m. | 4 a.m. | 5 a.m. | 6 a.m. | 7 a.m. | 8 a.m. | 9 a.m. | 10 a.m. | 11 a.m. | NOON |

The world is divided into 24 time zones; divisions are broadly 15° of longitude apart, and indicate a one-hour time difference from the neighboring zone. The Greenwich meridian, running through London, England, is the longitude from which the other calculations are made. Countries to the east are ahead of Greenwich Mean Time (GMT) and countries to the west are behind. The map shows the standard time across the

world at noon GMT. When a country straddles two time zones it may choose to have a standard time across the whole country that is midway between the two zones. For example, the standard time across India is five and a half hours ahead of GMT. The meridian that marks 12 hours ahead of GMT is the international date line, travelers crossing it move backward or forward by one calendar day.